Making DATA Work

THIRD EDITION

By Carol Kaffenberger, Ph.D.,
and Anita Young, Ph.D.

An ASCA National Model® Publication

AMERICAN
SCHOOL
COUNSELOR
ASSOCIATION

AMERICAN
SCHOOL
COUNSELOR
ASSOCIATION

ISBN 978-1-929289-46-2

The American School Counselor Association (ASCA) supports school counselors' efforts to help students focus on academic, personal/social and career development so they achieve success in school and are prepared to lead fulfilling lives as responsible members of society. ASCA, which is the school counseling division of the American Counseling Association, provides professional development, publications and other resources, research and advocacy to professional school counselors around the globe. For more information visit *www.schoolcounselor.org*.

Register your book at *www.schoolcounselor.org/MDW* to receive electronic copies of the activities and forms in "Making DATA Work (third edition)."

Table of Contents

Introduction

The purpose of this book is to provide school counselors with the tools to use data to develop, implement and evaluate their comprehensive school counseling program. This book provides step-by-step strategies to help school counselors identify and plan comprehensive school counseling programs based on program goals, implement accountability strategies and share results with stakeholders.

"Making DATA Work (third edition)" aligns with "The ASCA National Model: A Framework for School Counseling Programs (third edition)" and has been revised to reflect the changes in the most recent edition of the ASCA National Model. Data are a major element of the ASCA National Model. Data collection and analysis drive program planning, implementation and evaluation. This edition of "Making DATA Work" will provide school counselors with the necessary data management tools to help school counselors use data effectively.

The requirement to demonstrate research-based instruction to all students and make adequate yearly progress has been established with federal legislation such as Race to the Top Act of 2011, No Child Left Behind (2001) and the Individuals With Disabilities Education Act (2004). Similarly, the critical roles school counselors play in advancing student success, closing achievement and opportunity gaps and preparing students for college and career aspirations are equally important in the education reform movement (Dimmitt, Carey & Hatch, 2007; Dollarhide & Lemberger, 2006; McDonough, 2004).

Collecting and analyzing data can help school counselors and their administrators identify achievement gaps, understand educational issues and assess programs to ensure they are making a difference for all students. School counselors play a critical role in ensuring access and equitable educational choices are provided to all students (Bailey, Getch, & Chen-Hayes, 2007; Holcomb-McCoy, 2007). For school counseling programs to be considered a pivotal and valued resource to the learning environment, school counselors must commit to formulating and executing services that link their work to the instructional mission and concretely demonstrate accountability for student academic success (ASCA,

2012; Haycock, 2001; Brigman, Webb, & Campbell, 2007). Consequently, school counselors need to be able to recognize prevailing barriers causing students to struggle. The use of data to demonstrate impact and accountability assumes a wide base of knowledge, skill and application. Effective use of data skills can concretely link school counselors, and the school counseling program, to the academic achievement of all students and the outcome sought for connecting students to post-secondary options (Brooks-McNamara & Pederson, 2006; Dimmitt, 2009).

WHY DO SCHOOL COUNSELORS NEED TO USE DATA?

There are four purposes for using data:
1. Identify school counseling program goals
2. Monitor student progress to close the achievement gap
3. Assess and evaluate programs
4. Demonstrate school counseling program effectiveness.

Identify school counseling program goals: "Program goals define how the vision and mission will be accomplished and guide the development of the curriculum, small-group and closing-the-gap action plans" (ASCA, 2012, p. 25). School counseling program goals describe desired outcomes such as improved student achievement, attendance, behavior and safety. Program goals are based on an analysis of school data and align with the school's mission and school improvement plan.

> **EXAMPLE:** Seventh-grade students identified with two or more D/F grades in the first marking period will increase their GPA by 35 percent by the end of the semester.

Monitor student progress to close the achievement gap: Specific goals are identified based on an analysis of the school report card data and other school data to determine where achievement gaps exist. Using the school's student information system, school counselors identify students who are academically unsuccessful. Once achievement gaps are identified, goals are developed and the plan for achieving the goals is written. Developing targeted interventions for identified students will make data collection and analysis manageable.

[See page 21 for an example of the Manager Middle School data profile.]

> **EXAMPLE:** Ten students with one or more D/F on their November report card were selected to receive small-group counseling with the goal to decrease D's/F's by 25 percent.

Assess and evaluate programs. School counselors need to assess and evaluate the effectiveness of existing programs. School counselors should consider the following: Are existing programs achieving the goals for which they were intended? Do data exist to demonstrate existing programs are making a difference for students?

EXAMPLE 1: Evaluate the effectiveness of the school's mentoring program. Are students who are receiving mentoring making intended academic or personal/social gains?

EXAMPLE 2: Is there a need for an after-school homework club? Would a homework club increase student achievement?

Demonstrate school counseling program effectiveness: The last reason for using data is to demonstrate the effectiveness of the school counseling program. Sharing data with administrators, faculty and parents is an excellent way to educate stakeholders about the power of school counseling programs. Data can also be used to advocate for additional resources to increase program effectiveness. Analysis of the results of the school counseling program's goals should be part of the school counseling program evaluation. (See ASCA, 2012, p. 107 for program goal analysis suggestions.)

EXAMPLE: When Manager Middle School counselors collect data to show small-group counseling has reduced absenteeism and increased GPA for participating students, they are demonstrating that school counseling programs are effective and make a difference for students.

THE MAKING DATA WORK PROCESS

The school counselor's day is already full with the responsibilities of delivering a comprehensive program to all students. Determining how to collect data, when to begin the process and how to analyze results can be an even greater challenge. "Making DATA Work" is written to help school counselors get started and perfect the use of data to monitor student achievement and deliver a data-driven comprehensive school counseling program.

The process outlined in this book is just one way to get started. There are many excellent frameworks available to help professional school counselors understand the purposes of collecting data (Holcomb-McCoy, 2007; Rowell, 2005), to get started using data (Dimmitt et al., 2007; Gilchrist, 2007; Stone, & Dahir, 2007; Young & Kaffenberger, 2009) and to make sense of the data they collect (Poynton, & Baker, 2007). See References, Resources and Recommended Reading.

Throughout this book, examples of each step of the Making DATA Work process will be offered. An example of how one middle school counseling team applied the Making DATA Work process can be found on pages XX. Manager Middle School is a composite of many schools.

Making DATA Work is a four-step process, accomplished by working through a series of questions:
1. What is your goal?
2. How will you achieve it?
3. How will you analyze the data?
4. How will you use your results?

The fours steps of the process are: Design, Ask, Track, Announce (DATA).

THE MAKING DATA WORK PROCESS

Design: What is your goal?
- What is the gap, issue or student need you are addressing?
- How does addressing the issue affect student achievement, attendance, behavior and school safety?
- Is your goal based on existing data?
- Is there a "burning question" you should answer before identifying the goal?
- Is your goal specific, measurable, attainable, results-oriented and time-bound (SMART)?
- Does your goal align with the school's mission statement or school improvement plan?

Ask: How will you achieve the goal?
- What data do you need to examine to develop your SMART goal plan?
- Is the information or data available?
- What process, perception and outcome data will you collect and analyze?
- What procedures will you follow? What permissions, formal and informal, do you need? What are your action steps?
- Do you need to create data-collection instruments?
- What is your timeline for planning, collecting, analyzing and sharing the data?

Track: How will you analyze the data?
- How can you aggregate, collate or disaggregate the data to determine whether you have achieved your goal?
- Are you reporting process, perception and outcome data?
- How can you use technology to support the process?
- What do you learn from analyzing the data?
- How can you present the data so others can understand it?

Announce: How will you share your results?
- What do the results mean?
- How will you use the results?
- What are the implications of your results?
- What are the recommendations?
- With whom will you share the results?

DATA LITERACY SURVEY

Before beginning to read about how to implement the Making DATA Work process take the Data Literacy Survey to get a sense of where you are in your desire to use data to plan and implement your school counseling program.

ACTIVITY: **What is Your Data Literacy Score?**

What is your data literacy score? Complete the following quiz rating your use of data using the following key:

1 = Never   2 = Rarely   3 = Sometimes   4 = Often   5 = Always

1. _____ Do you examine school data regularly to make decisions about your programs and interventions?

2. _____ Are your school counseling interventions aligned with the school mission statement?

3. _____ Do you consider the school improvement plan when developing program goals?

4. _____ Do you collect data about all of the programs and school counseling curriculum activities you conduct?

5. _____ Can you create surveys to collect perception data?

6. _____ Do you know the difference among process, perception and outcome data?

7. _____ Do you analyze the data you collect?

8. _____ Do you share your findings with stakeholders (administrators, teachers, parents or students)?

9. _____ Do you conduct an annual school counseling program assessment?

10. _____ Do you identify goals that are specific, measurable, attainable, results-oriented and time-bound?

Total: _____

What is your data literacy score? Add your 10 individual scores to obtain your data literacy score.

Scoring:

41-50   You are a data-driven school counselor.
31-40   You believe collecting data is important and collect data regularly.
21-30   You would like to collect data but it doesn't always happen.
11-20   You are beginning to collect some data.
10   You are unsure of how to collect and use data.

Does this capture where you are? Would you like to increase your data competency? Is being a data-driven school counselor a goal of yours?

Ten Tips for Increasing Your Data Competency

1. Review school data reports over time to observe trends, changes and gaps.
2. Write a school counseling mission statement that aligns with the school's mission statement.
3. Review the school improvement plan, and consider how the school counseling program is contributing to schoolwide goals.
4. Collect pre- and post-test data from school counseling curriculum lessons and group counseling.
5. Evaluate schoolwide counseling programs to determine how they are helping students and/or how they can be improved or phased out.
6. Conduct a program audit once a year.
7. Set one to three SMART school counseling goals in August/September.
8. Share the data you collect with stakeholders.
9. Consider applying for Recognized ASCA Model Program (RAMP) status.
10. Consider how the data you are examining, collecting and sharing is serving students.

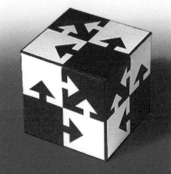

Design: What Is Your Goal?

CONNECTING DATA TO THE SCHOOL'S VISION AND MISSION

Data can help challenge status-quo thinking, reflect the equity of services, evaluate the range of belief systems and identify gaps (ASCA, 2012; Isaacs, 2003; Stone & Dahir, 2013). Vision and mission statements ground and provide direction for school counseling programs to develop one voice (ASCA, 2012). The ASCA National Model postulates that the foundation is the "what" of the program and is used to define what students should be able to do within the context of their learning environment. The vision and mission provide the school counseling program focus. School counselors seeking to design data-driven school counseling programs should build a foundation for their academic, career and personal/social services by creating vision and mission statements addressing the needs of all students (ASCA 2012; Carey, et al., 2005; Dahir & Stone, 2013). Beliefs about equitable student enrollment in rigorous courses, excessive tardiness, low student performance and high incidences of bullying and harassment are examples of courageous conversations to explore before framing the school counseling program mission (Singleton, & Linton, 2006). Linking the philosophical beliefs to the three broad domains and ASCA's National Standards for Student Competencies will help school counselors compose a mission statement that reflects one vision for a data-driven school counseling program.

ASCA (2012) recommends drafting a mission statement that:

- Aligns with the school's mission statement and may show linkages to district and state department of education mission statements
- Is written with students as the primary clients
- Advocates for equity, access and success of every student
- Indicates long-range results desired for all students (p. 24)

Future

VISION STATEMENT EXAMPLE:

Manager Middle School Vision Statement

The students at Manager Middle School are high-achieving students prepared for the challenges of high school and are career- and college-ready. The challenging curriculum and comprehensive school counseling program provided to all students offer the support they need to realize their full potential, become lifelong learners and make meaningful contributions to society.

Present

MISSION STATEMENT EXAMPLE:

Manager Middle School Mission Statement

Manager Middle School is committed to providing academic excellence in a safe, positive environment in which diversity is respected and all students feel invited and expected to become participants in their own academic, career, personal and social growth.

Once school counselors have developed a mission statement reflecting the school's vision, the next step is to consider the school counseling program goals. Program goals "define how the vision and mission will be accomplished and will guide the development of curriculum, small-group and closing-the-gap action plans" (ASCA, 2012, p. 25).

THE GOAL-SETTING PROCESS

Identifying a Burning Question

Sometimes it is necessary to investigate a burning question before implementing a school counseling activity or intervention to address an issue. Sometimes school counselors rush to identify an intervention to respond to a perceived need before fully understanding the underlying issues. The information gained will contribute to identifying a more focused intervention.

For instance, if school counselors are interested in increasing achievement among identified African-American students it will be important to understand the students' perception of what is contributing to their lack of success. The burning question might be: *Why is there a higher percentage of African-American students underachieving?*

Or before implementing new parenting programs to increase parent participation it would be important to collect data from parents to find out why they don't participate and what would encourage them to increase their participation. Burning question: *Why is parental participation at parent meetings declining?*

Answering the burning question is critical to the process of developing the right SMART goal and identifying the right intervention. Without understanding the issues, interventions and program activities may not address the real issues or contribute to accomplishing the goal.

BURNING QUESTION EXAMPLES:

- Is the mentoring program helping students meet or exceed higher standards?
- Does group counseling focusing on study skills help students improve standardized test scores?
- Are math scores increasing for students attending the after-school homework club?
- What are the factors causing academic failure or decline among third-grade students?
- Does small-group counseling with targeted sixth-graders having three or more discipline incidents reduce referrals?
- Why is ninth-grade absenteeism increasing at our high school?
- What are the perceptions of academically unsuccessful high school students concerning the supportive climate at their school?
- Why are females under-represented in advanced math classes?
- What is contributing to the increase in seventh grade discipline referrals?
- Does participation in the test anxiety small group increase the self-efficacy of student participants?
- Why is enrollment lowest in Advanced Placement/International Baccalaureate classes?

IDENTIFYING FOCUS AREAS AND PROGRAM GOALS

Review school data

Review school data such as the school report card. Data specific to each school can be found on the school, district and state websites. Are there achievement or opportunity barriers such as access to courses of rigor that may impede student success? What else do you need to know or understand to address these gaps?

See the example of how to review a school report card for Manager Middle School Data Profile, at the end of this section.

Conduct a school counseling program assessment

Consider how the school counseling program is addressing identified student needs through direct and indirect student services and whether data are collected and used to make program decisions.

> See "The ASCA National Model (third edition)," School Counseling Program Assessment, ASCA, 2012, pp. 59-62.

ACTIVITY: **Current school counseling activities and interventions**

Complete the brainstorming activity to create a picture of school counseling interventions and services and consider gaps in service provision (Bauman, 2004; Young & Kaffenberger, 2009).

To identify a focus and a program goal begin by listing all school counseling programs and interventions according to the ASCA domains to create an overview of the school counseling program. Consider how activities and interventions are addressing students' needs, providing equitable services and whether data have been collected to verify the effectiveness of the programs and opportunities.

Academic	Career	Personal/Social

Review the school improvement plan

Use the school improvement plan to consider how the school counselor can identify a goal aligned with one of the school improvement plan goals.

> **EXAMPLE:** A school improvement plan might identify increasing math achievement scores for an identified group of students. The school counselor could identify a similar achievement goal and support this academic goal by helping the group of students access after-school help, use a mentor, increase awareness of the importance of math and link to careers. In other words, by increasing positive attitudes toward math the school counselor may contribute to increasing math achievement.

Example of How School Counselors Contribute to Addressing the School Improvement Plan Goals

School Improvement Plan Goal	Teacher Evaluation Goal	School Counseling Program Goal	School Counseling Strategies
By June 2012, at least 50 percent of the Hispanic/Latino seventh-grade students enrolled in Math 7 will pass the state test at an advanced level.	By June 2013, 70 percent of identified students in my classes will pass the Math 7 state test at an advanced level.	By June 2013, identified Hispanic seventh-grade students will pass the Math 7 state test at an advanced level.	Small-group counseling Peer tutoring program Parent consultation Individual student planning meeting
By June 2013, graduation rate at Smith High School will increase from 89 percent in 2012 to 91 percent.	By June 2013, 90 percent of identified seniors in my classes will successfully complete all course work and be graduation-ready.	By June 2013, 90 percent of identified seniors will successfully complete all course work and be graduation-ready.	Three sessions of small-group counseling Individual student planning meetings Mentor tutoring program Parent consultation
By June 2013, 85 percent of fourth-graders will pass the state literacy test.	By June 2013, 95 percent of the students in my fourth-grade class will pass the state literacy test.	By June 2013, identified fourth-grade students will pass the state literacy test.	Small-group counseling Mentor tutor Parent education Individual counseling as needed

Based on a handout created by Valerie Hardy, 2013

Engage in a goal-setting activity

Engage in a goal-setting reflection activity with school counseling colleagues (Young & Kaffenberger, 2011). Consider the following questions:

- What is working at your school? What is helping students at your school to be successful?
- What are the barriers to student success at your school? What are you worried about?
- What school counseling programs or interventions address the issues you have identified?
- Is there a program goal resulting from this analysis?

ACTIVITY: **Goal-Setting Reflection**

What is working at your school? What is helping students at your school be successful?	What are the barriers to student success at your school? What are you worried about?
What school counseling programs or interventions address the identified issues?	What program goal results from this analysis? Is there a program goal resulting from this analysis?

Focusing Your Goal

In an effort to have a positive impact on all students, school counselors may be tempted to identify schoolwide or lofty goals. We encourage you to choose "one leaf" on the tree, not the whole forest. After identifying a worthy goal, give careful consideration to managing the amount of data by focusing on an identified program or target group and translating what you want to achieve into a measurable program goal. Ask if the goal is feasible and significant enough to contribute measurable knowledge. Ultimately, the purpose of monitoring data is to determine the impact on student success. Regardless of your goal, it will be important to connect its impact to outcome data.

Identifying a focused and specific goal will ensure achieving the goal will make a difference in the success of identified students, improve the efficiency of school counseling services or result in schoolwide systemic changes.

Questions for clarifying the focus and identifying a program goal:

- How will achieving the goal help students?
- What is the purpose of achieving the goal?
- What do you want to know and why?
- What are the educational implications of achieving the goal? How will the data be used to reduce barriers to learning or increase student achievement?
- What is the purpose of achieving the goal – to help students improve academics, behavior or attendance?
- How does addressing the issue relate to the school or school counseling program's mission statement or school improvement plan?

IDENTIFYING A SMART GOAL

Writing your goal using the SMART goal acronym will ensure your goal is specific, measurable, attainable, results-oriented and time-bound.

ACRONYM DEFINITION	EXAMPLES	
Specific: What is the issue, and is it based on data? The school counselor will identify a focus on a specific issue after a careful review of the data. Consider identifying a targeted group of students instead of the entire school or grade or class.	Elementary	Third-grade students with six or more absences
	Middle	Seventh-grade students with three or more discipline referrals in the first month of school.
	High	Seniors with one or more F grades on the first marking period report card

ACRONYM DEFINITION	EXAMPLES	
Measurable How will you evaluate the effectiveness of the intervention? For the goal to be measurable, you must identify the data you will be use to judge the goal's effectiveness before you implement the interventions.	Achievement	■ Grades and GPA ■ State testing ■ Graduation rate
	Attendance	■ Days absent ■ Tardies
	Behavior	■ Discipline referrals ■ Positive behavior interventions and support data
Attainable What outcome will be challenging to achieve but attainable? Identifying an attainable goal can seem like guess work. The school counselor should consider what can be achieved in one school year. What would be a goal that would stretch the school counseling team without being unattainable?	Elementary	Third-grade students will increase attendance by two days in the last grading period
	Middle	Seventh-grade students will decrease discipline referrals by 50 percent
	High	60 percent of seniors with one or more F grades will pass
Results-oriented What process, perception and outcome data will you report? SMART goal results are reported in terms of three types of data: ■ Process data – the number of students identified or the number of participants in an intervention ■ Perception data – describes attainment of competencies; changes in attitudes and beliefs; and perceived gains in knowledge data, what individuals think they know, believe or can do. ■ Outcome data – achievement, attendance, behavior or safety data	Elementary	49 percent of fifth-graders say they have been bullied. (Perception data)
	Middle	75 eighth-graders attended the information session (Process data)
	High	Average GPA for identified students was 2.3 (outcome data)

ACRONYM DEFINITION	EXAMPLES	
Time-bound When will the goal be accomplished? Typically SMART goals are achieved within the school year.	Elementary	Attendance goal will be measured at the end of the school year.
	Middle	Discipline referrals for first and fourth quarters will be measured.
	High	Senior year GPA will be calculated in June.

SMART GOAL EXAMPLES:

Identified ninth-grade students with one or more first-quarter F's will increase their GPA by 1.0 by the end of the school year.

Fourth-grade students with six or more absences in the previous school year will decrease absences by 50 percent by the end of the school year.

Eighth-grade students with three or more discipline referrals in the first quarter will reduce referrals by 75 percent by the end of the school year.

ACTIVITY: ## Write a School Counseling Program Goal

ABC High School counselors and administrators have reviewed their school data and realize the dropout rate has increased from 5 percent to 8 percent over the last four years, and the graduation rate decreased from 90 percent to 88 percent over a two-year timeframe. When looking at the dropout data they saw that Hispanic/Latino males were twice as likely to drop out as Caucasian males. To answer their burning question, "What were the causes of the increased dropout rate among Hispanic/Latino males?" the school counselors conducted focus groups with ninth-grade Hispanic/Latino male students. Focus group results indicated students did not correlate grades with post-secondary options or feel engaged with the school climate.

Write a SMART Goal:

Specific	
Measurable	
Attainable	
Results-oriented	
Time-bound	
Write your SMART goal	

Manager Middle School Data Profile

School Year	2011-12		2012-13		2013-14	
Enrollment	#	percent	#	percent	#	percent
Total Enrollment	930	100	920	100	940	100
Gifted School-Based	94	10.1	92	10	95	10
English for Speakers of Other Languages	140	15	170	18.4	182	19.4
Special Education Services	119	12.8	120	13	125	13.3

School Year	2011-12	2012-13	2013-14
Attendance Rate	percent	percent	percent
All Students	93	92	89
Asian or Pacific Islander	93	93	92
African-American/Black	91	90	90
Hispanic/Latino	89	89	87
White	95	95	94
Students with Disabilities	91	91	90
Students Identified as Disadvantaged	91	90	87
Limited English Proficiency Students	92	91	89

School Year	2011-12		2012-13		2013-14	
Ethnicity	#	percent	#	percent	#	percent
Asian or Pacific Islander	146	15.7	152	16.5	165	17.5
African-American/Black	311	33.4	292	31.73	269	28.6
Hispanic/Latino	198	21.25	250	27.17	301	32
White	275	29.56	226	24.56	205	21.8

School Year	2011-12		2012-13		2013-14	
Students with Disabilities	#	percent	#	percent	#	percent
All Students with Disabilities	119	100	120	100	125	100
Asian or Pacific Islander	21	17.6	19	15.8	19	15.1
African-American/Black	35	29.3	37	30.8	43	34.4
Hispanic/Latino	42	35.3	40	33.3	42	33.6
White	21	17.6	24	20	21	16.8

School Year	2011-12		2012-13		2013-14	
Economically Disadvantaged	#	percent	#	percent	#	percent
Yes	238	25.6	259	28.1	286	30.4

School Year	2011-12	2012-13	2013-14
School Safety	#	#	#
Weapons Offenses	6	5	8
Offenses Against Students	28	44	51
Offenses Against Staff	7	8	28
Alcohol, Tobacco, Drug Offenses	5	4	9
Disorderly or Disruptive Behavior	184	198	249
Technology Offenses	10	36	47

School Year	2011-12		2012-13		2013-14	
Percentage of Math State Assessment Scores* Seventh Grade	Passed	Tested	Passed	Tested	Passed	Tested
All Students	73	100	74	100	73	100
Ethnicity						
Asian or Pacific Islander	72	100	74	100	73	100
African-American/Black	69	99	71	99	71	99
Hispanic/Latino	67	99	71	99	69	99
White (Not of Hispanic Origin)	76	100	75	100	76	100
Students with Disabilities	69	99	66	99	63	99
Students Identified as Disadvantaged	66	99	67	99	67	99
Limited English Proficient Students	70	98	74	99	72	98

School Year	2011-12		2012-13		2013-14	
Percentage English State Assessment Scores* Seventh Grade	Passed	Tested	Passed	Tested	Passed	Tested
All Students	74	100	73	100	71	100
Ethnicity						
Asian or Pacific Islander	72	100	74	100	73	100
African-American/Black	69	99	70	99	70	99
Hispanic/Latino	67	99	67	99	69	99
White (Not of Hispanic Origin)	77	100	76	100	73	100
Students with Disabilities	70	99	66	99	70	99
Students Identified as Disadvantaged	69	99	65	99	69	99
Limited English Proficient Students	74	99	64	99	65	99

School Year	2011-12		2012-13		2013-14	
Percentage Math State Assessment Scores* Eighth Grade	**Passed**	**Tested**	**Passed**	**Tested**	**Passed**	**Tested**
All Students	76	100	75	100	75	100
Ethnicity						
Asian or Pacific Islander	80	100	81	100	82	100
African-American/Black	69	99	70	99	70	99
Hispanic/Latino	64	99	63	99	60	99
White (Not of Hispanic Origin)	77	100	76	100	75	100
Students with Disabilities	70	100	66	99	70	99
Students Identified as Disadvantaged	69	99	65	99	70	99
Limited English Proficient Students	74	99	64	99	63	99
*Pass rate for state accreditation for seventh-grade English is 74 percent.						
**Pass rate for state accreditation for eighth-grade math is 75 percent.						
Special Features: Block schedule; mentoring program; annual career day; after-school programs such as guitar club, art club, college partnership; homework achievers						

Data Analysis Activity

Review the report card data, and consider the following questions:

■ What is working well at this school?

■ What concerns you about these data?

■ Does an achievement gap exist? Describe.

■ What additional information do you need?

■ What is an appropriate focus? What data should you collect?

Examples of information that can be learned from reviewing the Middle School data profile include:

■ The percentage of math seventh-grade assessment scores for students with disabilities decreased 3 percent each year (69 percent – 66 percent – 63 percent) over a three-year timeframe.

■ There has been an increase in school safety offenses in all categories. For instance, technology offenses (e.g., cyberbullying) have increased from 10 to 47 offenses, an increase of 370 percent.

After reviewing the school data profile school counselors can take the following next steps:

■ What impact has the changing demographics had on the school climate, the state testing scores, attendance and safety issues at the school?

■ Do the school counselors need to collect additional data to understand the issue?

- What can the school counselors do to have an impact on the state testing gaps?
- Is the staff at this school prepared to work with a changing population of students, and is there anything the school counselors can do to facilitate this transition?
- Are students engaged? Do students believe the faculty is there to help them?
- Can school counseling goals be identified that are related to this data analysis?

Adapted from: Young, A., & Kaffenberger, C. (2009). Making data work. Alexandria, VA: American School Counselor Association. Reprinted in American School Counselor Association (2012). The ASCA National Model: A framework for school counseling programs (3rd. ed.) pp 109-111. Alexandria, VA: Author.

DESIGN EXAMPLES

The following design examples are offered for elementary, middle, high school and school counseling supervisors. These examples will be continued in each of the four steps of the Making DATA Work process.

DESIGN EXAMPLE 1:

Somewhere Elementary School
Design: What is the goal?

Approximately 40 percent of the 160 disciplinary referrals at Somewhere Elementary School are for misbehavior by sixth-graders.

The purpose: The school counselor wants to reduce or eliminate the number of sixth-grade referrals by the end of the school year. Before implementing group counseling with the sixth-grade students who have received more than three disciplinary referrals the school counselor will conduct a survey to understand the issue from the students' perspective. By asking the burning question, "Why do sixth-graders at this school account for 40 percent of the discipline referrals?" the school counselor hopes to have a better understanding of the issue and therefore increase the likelihood the intervention will be successful.

The mission of Somewhere Elementary School is "to create a caring and safe environment where all students can be academically successful." Therefore, understanding why 40 percent of the school's referrals are coming from the sixth grade is critical to the school's purpose.

The burning question: Why do sixth-graders at this school account for 40 percent of the discipline referrals?

The goal: Identified sixth-graders with three or more disciplinary infractions will decrease their infractions by 50 percent by the end of the school year.

Mistry Middle School

Design: What is the goal?

Approximately 10 percent of the students at Mistry Middle School are receiving failing grades at first interim. Ultimately the goal will be to increase achievement, but before the school counselors identify an intervention, they will survey the students to find out how effective they find the academic, personal and social support they receive.

The purpose: The school counselors want to know why these students are not successful and how to support and help them. They need to investigate the factors contributing to academic failure and student perception of the support they receive.

The mission of Mistry Middle School is "to partner with parents and community to provide a safe and challenging environment where all students are active participants in their learning." Therefore, understanding why 10 percent of the school's population is failing is critical to the school's goals.

The burning question: Do failing students report they receive effective academic, social and personal support at school?

The goal: Failing students with one or more F grades in the first quarter will have fewer F grades by the end of the school year.

Anywhere High School

Design: What is the goal?

Anywhere High School has the smallest high school student enrollment in its urban district. A critical aspect of the school's mission is to "instruct and assist all students to become independent thinkers and lifelong learners." Staff members are committed to fostering high standards, access and equity and college readiness for all students. Although their commitment is altruistic, ensuring career and college readiness to all students is a challenge. Student enrollment and retention is lowest in honors, AP/IB and dual-enrollment classes. Less than 30 percent of the total student population is enrolled in an honors, AP/IB or dual-enrollment course.

The purpose: Working collaboratively with administrators and teachers, the school counselors want to identify and eliminate barriers contributing to declining class enrollment in rigorous classes.

The burning question: Why is student enrollment lowest in honors, AP/IB and dual-enrollment classes at Anywhere High School?

Achievement High School
Design: What is the goal?

As the end of the school year approaches, the school counselor supervisor at Achievement High School is beginning to think about the department retreat and redefining goals for the upcoming school year. The school counseling department is committed to the use of data to effect change for all students. As a result, there have been schoolwide improvements in the areas of student achievement, attendance and engagement. Based on last year's recommendations, the department developed a new student transition program. What the department does not know is the impact of the new student transition program that was organized and implemented for the current school year. Ultimately it is hoped that the new transition program will have an impact on attendance and achievement.

The purpose: To measure the impact of the new transition program.

The goals: As a result of the ninth-grade transition program average GPA scores will be 0.4 points higher at the end of the school year as compared with last year. Attendance will increase during that same period by 2 percent.

DESIGN WORKSHEET

What is the gap, issue or student need you are addressing?

_____

_____

_____

How does addressing the issue affect student achievement, attendance, behavior and school safety?

_____

_____

_____

_____

Is your goal based on existing data?

_____

_____

_____

_____

Is there a burning question that should be answered before writing the goal?

_____

_____

_____

_____

Is your goal SMART?

_____

_____

_____

What is your goal?

_____

_____

_____

_____

PART II

Ask: How Will You Achieve the Goal?

Keys to Ask:

- What data do you need to develop your SMART goal?
- Is the information or data available?
- What process, perception and outcome data will you collect and analyze?
- What procedures will you follow? What approval, formal and informal do you need? What are the necessary action steps?
- Do you need to create data-collection instruments?
- What is your timeline for planning, collecting data, analyzing and sharing the data?

DATA NEEDED TO DEVELOP YOUR SMART GOAL

The first step, planning how to accomplish the goal, is critical to the success of the action research process. Consider the following questions in developing a plan:

- What information or data do you need to develop your SMART goal?
- Does the information or data currently exist?
- Where is this information or data located?
- Who owns it?
- What is the process to access the information?
- What approvals are needed?
- Who will be responsible for finding and gathering the data?
- Do you need to collect data to answer a burning question before identifying your SMART goal?

Use the school counseling program goal template to organize the process of planning your intervention, data collection and reporting procedures.

SCHOOL COUNSELING PROGRAM GOAL

School: _____   School Counselor(s): _____

DESIGN		ASK			TRACK	ANNOUNCE
SMART Goal	ASCA/State Student Standards	Existing Data	Action Steps	Timeline	Measure Effectiveness	Share Data With Others
					Process:	
					Perception:	
					Outcome:	

IS THE INFORMATION AVAILABLE?

Measuring goal achievement will involve the use of a variety of data-collection tools and strategies. Some data may already exist, such as the number of students in danger of failing, dropout rates, promotion and retention patterns and enrollment trends. In fact, much of what is needed to understand how to improve student achievement is already available and stored in district student information systems by gender, ethnicity, grade level and age. Gaining access and permission to use the data systems often depends on the district's policy concerning levels of authorization. Additional information, such as how long identified students have attended the school and what services are available to advance academic achievement and close achievement gaps, may also contribute to identifying the right SMART goal.

Examples of data that might be found in student information systems are found below.

Examples of Existing Data

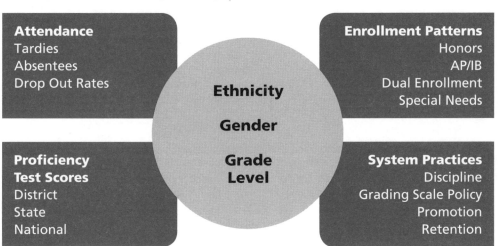

ANSWERING A BURNING QUESTION

Before identifying your goal you may need to answer a burning question to better understand the issue. For instance, to address the goal of improving achievement scores among African-American eighth-graders it may be helpful to survey the students to understand their perspective about what is contributing to low grades before setting the goal or identifying the intervention. In this case the Making DATA Work process is implemented in two phases. Phase one involves asking the question: "What are the factors contributing to identified students' poor grades?" Survey data could be collected from the students and possibly from teachers. After analyzing the results the SMART goal and intervention are identified in phase two.

Whether answering a burning question or identifying a program goal, data will need to be collected.

RESULTS

Results: What process, perception and outcome data will you be collecting and analyzing?

Another consideration is what results data you will need to collect and analyze. Results data include process, perception and outcome data that will be needed to assess whether the goal has been achieved and to improve or replicate the intervention. Every results report will require that these three types of data are collected and reported. It is important to consider what data answer the question and how you will collect them before implementing your intervention or program.

Description and examples of data

Types of Data	Description	Elementary Examples	Middle School Examples	High School Examples
Process	**The number of students involved in the program or intervention and a description of the activity**	35 fourth-graders participated in the six sessions of classroom lessons.	Eight seventh-graders participated in goal-setting group counseling.	325 students attended the college preparation program.
Perception	**Data describing what individuals think they know, believe or can do**	Fifth-grade students believed the conflict resolution unit helped them learn how to solve problems with peers.	65 percent of eighth-graders say they have observed bullying at school.	As a result of the group counseling intervention, students increased their knowledge of test-taking strategies by 75 percent.
Outcome	**Data showing the impact of the intervention or activity on student achievement, attendance and/or behavior**	Number of students identified in the red zone decreased by 40 percent by the end of the school year.	Average attendance for identified seventh-grade students increased from 78 percent to 84 percent.	86 percent of the senior class graduated, which is a 2 percent improvement from last year.

Identifying Types of Data

What type of data are each of the following? Process? Perception? Outcome?

1. _____O_____ The high school graduation rate has increased by 2 percent since 2012.

2. _Per_____ 95 percent of fourth-graders say they can identify a career goal.

3. _Pro_____ 57 eighth-graders attended the presentation.

4. _Per_____ 325 out of 523 (62 percent) seventh-graders believe being a bystander is wrong.

5. _____O_____ Discipline referrals at East Elementary School are down by 12 percent since last June.

6. _____O_____ 10 students in group counseling increased their GPA from 1.7 to 2.9 between the first and third marking period.

7. _Per_____ 60 percent of 10th-grade students at West High School say they do not complete homework.

8. _Pro_____ 33 second-graders participated in the getting along with others core curriculum unit.

9. _Pro_____ 98 percent of ninth-grade students completed a career plan by the end of the school year.

10. _____O_____ Identified fifth-grade students improved their report card work habit grades by an average of 40 percent.

1. Outcome 2. Perception 3. Process 4. Perception 5. Outcome 6. Outcome 7. Perception 8. Process 9. Process 10. Outcome

DATA-COLLECTION METHODS

After identifying the type of data to examine, the next step is to determine the method you will use to collect the data. Answering a burning question is a form of action research (Fraenkel & Wallen, 2009; Gillies, 1993; Guiffrida, 2011; Young & Kaffenberger, 2009). Researchers use three methodologies to address educational issues: quantitative, qualitative and mixed methodology (Denzin & Lincoln, 2011; Patton, 2002; Schwandt, 2007).

Quantitative data are most often collected when the variable or elements are measured along a scale. The data differ in amount or degree, along a continuum from less to more and may be reduced to numerical scores or percentages. Data collection frequently occurs via questioning participants to complete the scale in the form of a survey. Quantitative research also focuses on objective statistical outcomes measuring student achievement (Rubin, 2008).

Qualitative data collection occurs in narrative description. Collecting qualitative data is also a legitimate way to understand educational issues. Qualitative data can be gathered in a variety of ways: open-ended questions included on a survey, interviews and focus groups. Students' stories can characterize an issue in useful ways and through relevant data elements. The combination of both methodologies is referred to as a mixed methodology.

Questions to consider when deciding on data collection methods:
- Do the data already exist?
- How will the data be collected?
- What type of results data, process, perception and outcome will be identified?
- Will data be gathered using quantitative, qualitative or both methods?
- Will surveys be developed? Pre-tests or post-tests used?
- Will a focus group be facilitated? Or an interview conducted?
- Will participant observations be necessary?

How Data are Collected

Type of Data	How Data are Collected	Example
Process	Keep track of number of participants, number of sessions in a log.	Take attendance before each classroom lesson, and log the number of lessons provided. Sign-in sheet before a large-group activity Simple count
Perception	Data are collected using surveys, pre- and post-tests, program evaluation surveys, needs assessment surveys or opinion surveys. Survey data can be collected electronically or using paper copies.	Needs assessment was conducted to understand 11th-graders' concerns about college-going before the college preparation sessions were planned. Pre- and post-test data were collected before and after the small-group counseling with seventh-grade students to understand their test-taking concerns and to evaluate how students believe the school counseling program has helped them.
Outcome	Reports from the student information system are analyzed (e.g., grades, attendance, discipline reports, state testing results).	Graduation rate from the previous year is compared with graduation rate in the current year. Attendance data for identified students are examined at the end of the first marking period and compared with the attendance data in the final marking period. GPA for identified students is compared before and after the group counseling intervention.

**What type of results data do you need to collect
to achieve this program goal?**

Program Goal:
Identified ninth-grade students will increase their first-quarter GPA by an average of 1.0
point by the end of the school year..

What process data do you need to gather?

• participation
- report cards
- attendance/discipline records

What perception data do you need to collect?

• survey - importance of school/grades
• end of year report card
• survey - student feelings about why they
are struggling

What outcome data will demonstrate that the goal is achieved?

• RC BOY vs EOY report card

WHAT PROCEDURES WILL YOU FOLLOW?

Once you have identified your program goal it is critical that you think through the procedures for identifying actions steps that might include: inviting stakeholders; gaining permissions; identifying data-collection procedures; collecting, organizing and reporting the findings. Here is a checklist of action-planning steps.

Checklist of Action-Planning Steps

Suggested Action-Planning Steps	Date	Completed
Invite stakeholders to participate in the process		
Create data collection instruments, such as surveys		
Gain approval, formal and informal, to conduct data collection		
Align procedures with the school counseling calendar and instructional planning		
Identify school counseling interventions		
Identify data-collection strategies and obstacles		
Organize and disaggregate data (e.g., grades, attendance, standardized tests, surveys)		
Consider how you will use the results		
Create a results report		
Share results with administrators and other stakeholders		

Action Steps for SMART Goal Plan

October: Administrator asks the school counselors to help decrease the high percentage of the discipline referrals from sixth-grade students; school counselors gather demographic descriptive data concerning the number of referrals per student, gender, types of infractions, time of day, race/ethnicity, special education/English-language learners.

November: After reviewing the data the school counselors identify a SMART goal in collaboration with the administrative leadership team. SMART Goal: Discipline referrals for identified sixth-grade students will be reduced from 40 percent to 15 percent by the end of the school year. Survey data will be gathered from students and teachers to determine intervention. Identified students (students with three or more referrals) will work with school counselors individually and in small groups January through May.

December: Intervention plan will begin.

January–May: School counselors will work with students and monitor progress by asking teachers for input about behavior periodically. School counselors will monitor discipline referrals and make adjustments to intervention as needed.

February: The school counselors will have students and teachers take a post-test survey to gather perception data about the success of the intervention.

May: Outcome data, the number of referrals for identified students will be calculated. Pre- and post-test survey data will be analyzed. Results will be shared and discussed with the administrative team and faculty. Recommendations will be made.

APPROVALS NEEDED

If using existing data, determine how to get access to the data and what approval is needed. This may require getting approval from administrators and stakeholders. This approval may be as informal as verbal administrative approval or may require district human subject review board approval, particularly if you plan to publish the results. Share data-gathering goals and procedures with teachers and administrators to increase involvement and buy-in.

Gaining Approval and Access
- Review data-collection procedures with administrators to determine what permissions, if any, are required.
- Consider including stakeholders (students, teachers, administrators) in the process.
- Seek district approval if required.
- Obtain written permission from parents, if required by district policy, to survey or interview students or if they participate in a focus group.

CREATING DATA-COLLECTION INSTRUMENTS

- Do you need to create data-collection instruments, such as pre- and post-test surveys, needs assessments, evaluation surveys, focus group questions?
- Who will create the instruments?
- How will you check for usefulness and clarity of the instruments?
- Will you field-test the instrument prior to administering to a large group?

Achieving the goal may require the development of additional data-collection tools. For instance, to gain student and teacher opinions about the burning question, school counselors could develop a survey. Surveys can be administered in large or small quantity, via postal mail or electronically. One-page format surveys with specific directions, limited statements, age-appropriate questions and common language are user-friendly and produce higher response rates (Denzin & Lincoln, 2011). The disadvantage of surveys occurs when statements are ambiguous without chance for explanation. Surveys should have, at minimum, face validity, meaning every question should be appropriate for the purpose intended.

Creating a Survey

Surveys are used to collect perception data. Perception data measure perceived attainment of competencies, perceived attitudes and beliefs and perceived knowledge. Post-tests administered after an intervention measure changes in attitudes, beliefs or knowledge.

There are four types of surveys school counselors use (ASCA, 2012, p. 51):

Pre-Post	Pre-post surveys are given before and after an intervention to measure perceived knowledge gained or a change in perception
Needs Assessment	Needs assessments are given to students or stakeholders to gather perception of student or program needs.
Evaluation	Evaluation surveys are given to participants after an intervention or activity to gather opinions about the value of the intervention or activity.
Opinion	Opinion surveys are given to students or stakeholders to understand their perception of the school counseling program or school counseling activities.

Surveys can be used for pre- and post-tests to determine the impact of change in knowledge or behavior as a result of an intervention. Surveys can also be used to gather perception data, such as student attitudes toward school, the need for a mentoring program or student experiences with bullying.

Surveys can be used to gain information that will contribute to understanding the issue, answering the burning question. For instance, before writing a SMART goal and identifying an intervention to help failing students, collecting perception data from students may help answer the burning question, "How do students at ABC High School explain the factors contributing to student failure?"

Survey Development Tips

- Use a simple one-page format with the fewest possible questions.
- Be sure that your survey has high face validity, meaning that all of the items clearly relate to the question you are trying to answer. Have a clear purpose in mind. What is it that you want to learn or need to know or understand? Every question should be related to your purpose.
- Use parallel language that requires a response to a positive or negatively phrased statement. Do not mix these types of questions. This is an example of two positively stated parallel statements: "I know how to solve problems with friends," "I am helpful."
- Conduct pre- and post-surveys of workshops, school counseling curriculum lessons, programs and groups, and compare the results.
- Administer surveys at the beginning to assess knowledge (what do the students already know) and the end to assess learning (how the program/unit has been benefited the student).
- Consider providing space for one or two open-ended questions.

Response Scales

Asking participants to complete a survey and respond using a scale allows the researcher to convert the response to a numerical scale and easily analyze the data. For example, if respondents were asked to use a four-point scale (e.g., strongly disagree, disagree, agree, strongly agree) to answer the question: "I know how to access financial aid for college" their responses would be converted to a numerical scale: strongly disagree=1, disagree=2, agree=3, strongly agree=4).

Be sure to develop a consistent response scale such as a three-point scale (e.g., never, sometimes, always), five-point scale (e.g., strongly disagree, disagree, unsure, agree, strongly agree), four-point scale (e.g., strongly disagree, disagree, agree, strongly agree) or a two-point scale (yes, no). Clearly state in the directions how to answer the questions, and explain the survey's purpose. Starting with anonymous fact-finding questions and progressing to opinion-based questions is more likely to engage respondents. If time and space permit, consider probing questions about the scale responses such as, "If you strongly agree or disagree, please comment." Ending the survey with feedback requests about the survey can help develop future surveys or expand the current one.

Although surveys produce quantitative data, structured or semi-structured interview questions asked during focus groups or individual interviews give voice to the data through qualitative responses. Structured and semi-structured interview questions consist of a sequence of predetermined questions asked to all respondents in the same way. Interviewing a sample of the identified population increases the salience of questions and allows further probing and the emergence of observations. Similar to quantitative data collections, oral interview questions should be feasible and the interview process timely. Additionally, interviewers should be knowledgeable about facilitating groups.

For young children, consider using animated responses such as smiling and frowning faces or simple yes/no responses.

Two-point scale example:

I like school.	Yes	No
I am good at math.	Yes	No

For older children, consider using a Likert scale, 1 to 3, 1 to 4 or 1 to 5, and link the number value to its meaning. For example, 1 is strongly disagree, 2 is disagree, 3 is unsure, 4 is agree and 5 is strongly agree.

Three-point scale example:

	Rarely	Sometimes	Often
I ask questions in class when I do not understand.	1	2	3
I do my homework.	1	2	3
I study for tests.	1	2	3

Four-point scale example:

	Strongly Disagree	Disagree	Agree	Strongly Agree
I have friends at school.	1	2	3	4
When I have a problem, I talk to my friends.	1	2	3	4
When I have a problem, I talk to my parents.	1	2	3	4

Five-point scale example:

	Strongly Disagree	Disagree	Unsure	Agree	Strongly Agree
I understand the ASCA National Model.	1	2	3	4	5
I use data to demonstrate program effectiveness.	1	2	3	4	5

Use parallel language so participants are asked to respond to positive or negative statements. For example, "New students at this school do not feel welcome" would be a negative statement. "New students at this school feel welcome" would be a positive version of the same statement.

Consider providing space for one or two open-ended questions to gain additional information.

Conduct pre- and post-tests for school counseling curriculum lessons, small groups, presentations, workshops and programs. Administer at the beginning to assess knowledge and at the end to assess learning.

ACTIVITY: **Practice Designing a Survey**

DESIGN

A group of seventh-grade boys at Tucker Middle School has been identified because of low grades and poor behavior. Before implementing an intervention the school counselor decides to collect perception data.

Burning Question: What are the perceptions of seventh-grade students about what will help them improve their grades and behavior?

ASK

- Develop a five-item survey you will use to develop an intervention (e.g., group counseling) based on the students' perceptions.
- Provide the directions for completing the survey.
- Determine the response scale, and ask an open-ended question.

Directions:

_____

_____

1. _____

_____

2. _____

_____

3. _____

_____

4. _____

_____

5. _____

_____

Open-ended question:_____

_____

_____

PARTICIPANT SELECTION AND SAMPLE SIZE

Keep in mind that the purpose of practitioner research is to improve services to students; therefore sample selection may not be a relevant factor. In other words gaining the insights from all eight members of a small counseling group will both inform practice and contribute to understanding students' particular needs. Other times hearing from all members of a group will be essential. Decisions about participant selection and sample size should be based of the consideration of what data will help answer the burning question or achieve the goal.

There may be times when deciding who to survey and the sample size will be important to consider. When trying to understand the beliefs of a large group, such as a high school population, it is important to consider whether the sample size will produce significant responses to answer the burning question or achieve the goal. The sample size should provide an accurate representation of how the larger group refers to the applicable population. If the question targets a small population, then a 100 percent sample size is conceivable. Convenience samples are individuals who are (conveniently) available to answer the question. Convenience samples may not be representative of the population (Fraenkel & Wallen, 2000). Purposive samples, unlike convenience samples, are selected based on prior information and are believed to provide the data needed. Various random samples exist; the most common, simple random sample is one in which every individual has an equal and independent chance of selection. To address a question involving a large number of respondents, a simple random sampling of the population increases the probability that any respondent selected to answer the survey is equal to all members of the population.

EXAMPLE 1:

Answering a burning question

Question: What are the factors contributing to poor school attendance at Manager Middle School?

Target population: Students attending Manager Middle School

Random sample: All students with three or more absences and equal chance of selection

Purposive sample: Students with three or more absences in ninth grade

Convenient sample: Student with three or more absences and available to complete the survey

Achieving a program goal

Program goal: Students with six or more absences in the first marking period will reduce the average number of absences by 35 percent in the final marking period.

Target population: 19 students had six or more absences in the first marking period

Purposive sample: Collect data from all 19 students

Convenient sample: In this case collecting data from all 19 students is the only way to know whether the goal is achieved because the population is small.

FOCUS GROUPS AND INTERVIEWS

Qualitative research data collection draws from multiple sources and provides the power and voice to determine which and when data become collectable (Denzin & Lincoln, 2011). Just as with quantitative design, the foundation for framing a successful qualitative research design utilizing interviews begins with the selection of a topic of interest that evolves the burning question. Focus groups and interviews are major categorical approaches to qualitative inquiry (Schwandt, 2007).

There are several types of interviews and methods of interviewing participants such as mail, electronic, telephone, face-to-face and group. One of two common methods, individual interviews, also known as participant observation, involves one-on-one verbal exchange. Individual interviews, as with focus groups, vary according to purpose and are most effective when studying opinions, perceptions and practices.

A second method, face-to-face group interviews, more commonly known as focus groups, is frequently used to predict and analyze opinions, progress and educational value (Denzin & Lincoln, 2011). The term applies to situations in which the interviewer asks specific questions about a topic for the purpose of collective and collaborative research centering on multiple voices of participants.

Focus groups and interviews are excellent ways to collect information about issues under investigation. Bringing a small group of stakeholders together to conduct a focused discussion is a productive way to understand the perspective of students, faculty or parents. Interviewing individual stakeholders is also a useful way to gather insider information about the issue. Here are some tips for facilitating focus groups or conducting interviews.

Tips for Facilitating Focus Groups and Conducting Interviews:

- Focus groups are conducted with a group ranging in number from two to 10.
- Establish procedures in advance, deciding if you will audio or video tape, if you need permission to tape and who will take notes.
- Consider having two facilitators lead the group.
- Develop an interview guide.
- Articulate group rules.
- Determine exact wording and sequence of questions in advance.
- Probe for clarity if needed.
- Respect respondents' answers.

Example of Procedures for Focus Groups

Script for Focus Groups:

Interviewer: Good afternoon, and welcome to the MISTRY focus group. Thank you for consenting to participate in this action research project designed to improve the academic success of [targeted population]. Focus group dialogue will be recorded and transcribed for factual interpretation. Data collected will be used to: (indicate how data will be used)

1. Improve student attendance.
2. Decrease number of students on the D/F list, etc.
3. Provide feedback that will improve classroom instruction.
4. Help all students succeed.
5. Collaborate with educational stakeholders.
6. Close achievement gaps.

Before we begin, I want to confirm that you have signed the consent form, fully understand the purpose of the research and voluntarily participate. Do you have any questions or comments?

Ground Rules:

This is strictly an action research project that will be audio taped and/or video taped so we do not miss any comments. Please speak clearly, and allow only one person to speak at a given time. If several people are talking at the same time, the tape will be garbled, and we will miss your comments. We will be on a first-name basis; however, pseudonyms will be attached to the transcribed data. We will keep your responses confidential, and we ask that you not share others' responses outside the group. Please provide candid and honest comments.

Tips:

1. Ask participants to write their answers on note cards prior to beginning the discussion.
2. Use poster boards to record group answers.
3. Start with an icebreaker-type question.

EXAMPLES OF ASK

ASK EXAMPLE 1:

Somewhere Elementary School
Ask: How will you achieve your goal?

Record review: The school counselor, teachers and administration will analyze the sixth-grade discipline referrals, addressing the following areas:

School Demographics
- 850 students at enrolled grades K-6
- 130 sixth-graders

Discipline Referral Stats
- 160 referrals
- 40 percent of all referrals in sixth grade = 64 sixth-grade referrals

Sixth-Grade Faculty = 14 Teachers
- Five classroom teachers
- Two school counselors
- Two music teachers
- Two LD teachers/resource
- Two P.E. teachers
- One computer lab teacher

Sixth-Grade Referral Student Demographics
- 64 referrals total for sixth grade
- 28 sixth-grade students referred three or more times
- Two students received six

- Four students received five
- Nine students received four
- 13 students received three
- 25 students received one or two

Type of Referrals

Type		
Bus incident referrals	17	27%
Teacher/classroom referrals	26	40%
Playground referrals	9	14%
After school (walking home) reports	4	6%
Hallway referrals	8	13%

Student Demographics for 28 Identified Students
- 20 male, eight female
- 11 African-American, seven Hispanic, 10 Caucasian
- 64 percent of the 28 (18) students with one or more failing grade

Student survey: To understand why students are getting in trouble, the school counselor will develop a student survey and administer it to all sixth-grade students who have received three or more disciplinary referrals.

Faculty survey: To understand why students are getting in trouble, the school counselor will develop a survey and give it to all faculty who work with the sixth-graders.

Intervention will be developed based on input from surveys and analysis of the type of discipline referrals.

Mistry Middle School

Ask: How will you achieve your goal?

The school counselors will collect and organize demographic information describing the target population.

Demographic information: grade, gender, race/ethnicity, free/reduced lunch, special education designation, English-language learner designation, previous grades, standardized testing and standardized test results will all help to identify and describe the target population. What is not known is why students are failing and whether there are school climate issues affecting these students.

To understand why students are receiving D/F grades and if school climate has any bearing on these students' grades, the school counseling department will develop a survey to give to all 50 identified students with D/F grades. The survey will ask students who received D/F grades about their perception of the academic support they receive at school and at home.

Timeline:

November: Concerns about the D/F students will be discussed with the administration, the school counseling department and grade-level teams.

December: The school counseling department will gather and disaggregate demographic information and develop, test and share the survey with administrators.

January: Parent permission will be sought to complete survey. The purpose of the survey will be shared with students, and it will be given to students to complete during group advisement period. Data will be organized and presented to faculty for discussion; recommendations resulting from the data will be developed.

February: Two remedial activities/strategies agreed upon by school counselors, administrators and teachers will be implemented during the third and fourth marking periods.

Data at the end of the year will be collected and compared with September data.

Anywhere High School
Ask: How will you achieve your goal?

Considering the school's mission statement and small population, school counselors will seek answers from a random sample of all current ninth- through 11th-grade students. By doing so, retention information is gained from currently enrolled students, and enrollment data from students who are not enrolled can also be assessed.

Record review: Demographic information such as gender, race/ethnicity, free/reduced lunch, special education designation, English-speaking students of other languages, previous grades, standardized testing and state test results will help to identify and determine the profile of currently enrolled students.

Student survey: To understand why student enrollment is lowest in honors, AP/IB and dual-enrollment classes, the school counseling department will administer a student survey to a random sample of ninth- through 11th-grade students prior to academic advisement/registration orientations for the upcoming school year. The survey will consist of Likert-scaled statements relating to barriers prohibiting the selection and retention of rigorous course selections. Results will be used to increase access and maintain equity, as well as initiate retention strategies for currently enrolled students.

Timeline:
October: School counselors will talk with stakeholders to clarify issues and develop appropriate survey statements. They will disaggregate demographic information. School counselors will seek administrative approval and determine the survey dissemination method.

November–December: School counselors will request parent permission to administer the survey, share the purpose of the survey with students and administer the survey. Data will be organized and disaggregated.

January: Results will be presented to the administration and faculty respectively for discussion; systemic strategies will be developed.

February–April: Recommended enrollment strategies will be implemented during academic advisement and registration orientations for the upcoming school year. A school task force will meet to discuss barriers and recommend retention strategies.

May: Retention strategies will be finalized and ready for implementation at the beginning of the upcoming school year.

School Counselor Supervisor at Achievement High School

Ask: How will you answer your question?

Review school improvement plan: Review the new student orientation program to confirm alignment with the school's mission and accountability goals.

Record review: Collect demographic information about new student class enrollment patterns, attendance data, club/activities participation and behavioral referrals on the students who participated in the new student orientation program.

Evaluate pre- and post-test results: Collect pre- and post-test evaluative results from school counselors and other individuals who facilitated activities.

Focus group: In addition to reviewing the aforementioned data, a focus group consisting of members of the advisory council and new students will be invited to review the data and discuss the issue. Procedures will be established in advance. An interview guide will ensure all members are asked the same questions.

Timeline:
One month timeline

ASK WORKSHEET

What data do you need to examine to develop your SMART goal plan?

_____

_____

_____

Is the information or data available?

_____

_____

_____

_____

What process, perception and outcome data will you be collecting and analyzing?

_____

_____

_____

_____

What procedures will you follow?

_____

_____

_____

_____

Do you need to create data-collection instruments?

_____

_____

_____

What is your timeline for planning, collecting, analyzing and sharing the data?

_____

_____

_____

_____

Track: How Will You Analyze the Data?

Once the data are collected it's time to organize them in a way that answers the burning question or helps determine whether your goal was achieved. Analyzing data is sometimes the most difficult step to tackle. Here are some suggestions for simplifying the process of organizing and analyzing data.

ORGANIZING AND REPORTING THE DATA

There are three types of data you will need to collect: process, perception and outcome data. Collecting, organizing and reporting each of these types of data require different strategies.

Process data are reported simply by stating the number of participants and number of sessions.

Perception data are generally collected using surveys. Aggregating survey data and finding simple ways to represent your data are the first steps in analyzing the data.

Outcome data are achievement, behavior/discipline or attendance data. Collecting outcome data usually involves accessing student information systems that retain this type of student data. Analyzing student data may involve comparing scores before or after an intervention.

AGGREGATING PERCEPTION DATA

There are two simple ways to analyze data from surveys based on two-, three-, four- or five-point Likert scales.

Finding the Average

One way to organize the data is to find the average score for each question. The average score is also referred to as the mean. To find the average, or mean, begin by assigning a number to each response on the scale (e.g., "no"=1; "unsure"= 2; "yes"=3).

For example:

Sixteen students were asked to complete a survey responding on a three-point scale – always, sometimes, never. When using a three-point scale, let never=1, sometimes=2 and always=3.

The first question was: Do you regularly complete assigned homework?

Calculate the average score for this question.
Sixteen students answered this survey item as follows: Three students answered "never." Three students chose "sometimes," and 10 students chose "always."

The total score would be:

3 (students) X 1 (never) + 3 (students) X 2 (sometimes) + 10 (students) X 3 (always)

3 + 6 + 30 = 39

Divide the total number (39) by the number of students (16)

39/16 = 2.4

In other words the average score for this question was 2.4, meaning students answered midway between "sometimes" and "always" to the question about completing homework. So these students, for the most part, do their homework.

Finding the Percent

Another way to organize the data is to find the percent. Percent indicates what part of the total group accomplished the identified task. To find the percent begin with the total group.

For example:

If 125 students (part of the group) graduated from Fortune High School out of a possible graduating class of 143 students (total group):

125/143 = 87 percent

In other words, out of a class of 143 students, 87 percent of the class graduated. The percent helps us compare the graduation rate at Fortune High School with the graduation rate at other schools and compare graduation rates over time.

EXAMPLE: Using Averages and Percents

Consider another example describing how you would take the responses of students on a pre- and post-test and convert their scores to averages that can then be compared.

Before conducting a six-week series of lessons on study skills for sixth-graders, 50 students completed a four-question pre-test.

To calculate the average, begin by making a tally sheet where you keep track of the number of responses for each category (never, rarely, often, always).

Pre-Test Scores (50 students responded in the following ways)

	Never (1)	Rarely (2)	Often (3)	Always (4)
I do my homework.	20	17	6	7
I study for tests.	25	14	6	5
I read every night.	22	11	7	10
I organize my bookbag every night.	27	14	7	2

Calculate the average by multiplying the number of respondents by the number you've assigned to the answer.

Question 1: I do my homework.
20 x 1 = 20 (20 students answered "never" – 1)
17 x 2 = 34 (17 students answered "rarely" – 2)
6 x 3 = 18 (6 students answered "often" – 3)
7 x 4 = 28 (7 students answered "always" – 4)
20 + 34 + 18 + 28 = 100
100/50 = 2.0

So the average score for question one is 100 divided by 50 (number of respondents) = 2.0 In other words, an average student response to this question is 2.0 = "rarely." The average of student responses is that they rarely do homework.

Question 2: I study for tests.
25 x 1 = 25 (25 students answered "never")
14 x 2 = 28
6 x 3 = 18
5 x 4 = 20
25 + 28 + 18 = 20 = 91
91/50 = 1.82
The average for student responses to the question of whether they study for tests, 1.82, is slightly lower than "rarely."

Question 3: I read every night.

22 x 1 = 22 (22 students answered "never")
11 x 2 = 22
7 x 3 = 21
10 x 4 = 40
22 + 22 + 21 + 40 = 105
105/50 = 2.1

The average for student responses to the question of about nightly reading is right above "rarely."

Your turn: what is the average for the final question?
Question 4: I organize my bookbag every night.

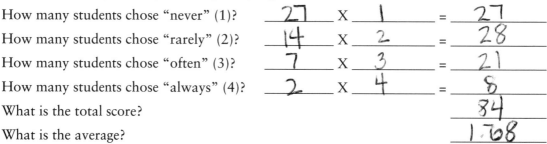

How many students chose "never" (1)?	27	X 1	= 27
How many students chose "rarely" (2)?	14	X 2	= 28
How many students chose "often" (3)?	7	X 3	= 21
How many students chose "always" (4)?	2	X 4	= 8
What is the total score?			84
What is the average?			1.68

Summary of Pre-Test Scores and Averages

	Never (1)	Rarely (2)	Often (3)	Always (4)	Average
I do my homework.	20	17	6	7	2.00
I study for tests.	25	14	6	5	1.82
I read every night.	22	11	7	10	2.10
I organize my bookbag every night.	27	14	7	2	1.68

These perception data represent what students think they know or can do before the intervention. These data will help the school counselor structure the intervention.

USING PERCENTS

Sometimes it is important to know the percent of students who respond in a particular way to the question. In other words, rather than knowing the average response score is 2.0, it might be more important to know that 40 percent of students never do homework and only 14 percent always do homework.

You can also calculate the percent of students who responded to each category by dividing the number of respondents in the category by the number of total respondents; for example, the number of students responding to the question (part of the whole) divided by the total number of students (the whole group).

E.g., Divide 20 students (part of the total group that responded "never do homework") by 50 students (the whole group that took the survey). 20/50 = 0.4 x 100 = 40 percent. In other words, 40 percent of the whole group say they never do homework.

Pre-Test Scores

	Never	Rarely	Often	Always
I do my homework.	20 40 percent	17 34 percent	6 12 percent	7 14 percent
I study for tests.	25 50 percent	14 28 percent	6 12 percent	5 10 percent
I read every night.	22 44 percent	11 22 percent	7 14 percent	10 20 percent
I organize my bookbag each night.	27 54 percent	14 28 percent	7 14 percent	2 4 percent

After you've presented the school counseling curriculum unit, re-administer the same test, calling it a post-test, and go through the same process for calculating the scores. The hope is that the average scores will go up and that as a result of your school counseling curriculum lessons students will have better study skills and that a higher percent of students are doing homework, studying for tests, reading and organizing bookbags.

Post-Test Scores

	Never	Rarely	Often	Always	Average
I do my homework.	3	2	8	37	3.60
I study for tests.	2	5	19	24	3.30
I read every night.	4	6	10	30	3.35
I organize my bookbag each night.	5	4	20	21	3.14

Question 1: I do my homework.
3 x 1 = 3
2 x 2 = 4
8 x 3 = 24
37 x 4 = 148
3 + 4 + 24 + 148 = 180
180/50 = 3.6

Question 2: I study for tests.
2 x 1 = 2
5 x 2 = 10
19 x 3 = 57
24 x 4 = 96
2 + 10 + 57 + 96 = 165
165/50 = 3.30

Question 3: I read every night.
4 x 1 = 4
6 x 2 = 12
10 x 3 = 30
30 x 4 = 120
4 + 12 + 30 + 120 = 166
166/50 = 3.35

Question 4: I organize my bookbag every night.
5 x 1 = 5
4 x 2 = 8
20 x 3 = 60
21 x 4 = 84
5 + 8 + 60 + 84 = 157
157/50 = 3.14

Pre-Test and Post-Test Summary

	Pre-Test	Post-Test
Question 1	2.00	3.60
Question 2	1.82	3.30
Question 3	2.10	3.35
Question 4	1.68	3.14

We can see that student perception of their study skills has increased as a result of the intervention. On question one, "I do my homework," the average student response is now between "sometimes" and "always" and has increased by 1.60. This is good information, but we might want to calculate the percent of change to understand the impact of the intervention on student perception about doing homework.

WORKING WITH THE PERCENT CHANGE

It is obvious from the chart comparing the pre- and post-test scores that the average of students' responses has increased, but to measure the amount of growth you will want to calculate the percent of change between the two sets of scores.

Calculating the Percent Change:
Final # (b) – beginning # (a) = change (c)
Change (c)/beginning # (a) X 100 = percent change
c/a = d x 100 = percent change

Apply the formula using the example for question one:
(post-test average) 3.60 – 2.00 (pre-test average) = 1.60 (change)

1.60 (change)/2.00 (per-test average) X 100 = 80 percent

In other words students reported an 80 percent increase in their homework completion since participating in the school counseling curriculum unit.

> **ACTIVITY:** **Calculate the percentage of change for questions two, three and four.**

Question 2: I study for tests.

Final average score _3.3_ minus beginning average score _1.82_ = change _1.46_

Change _1.46_ divided by beginning score _1.86_ X 100 = percent change _78.5%_

Question 3: I read every day.

Final average score _3.35_ minus beginning average score _2.1_ = change _1.21_

Change _1.21_ divided by beginning score _2.1_ X 100 = percent change _57.6%_

Question 4: I organize my bookbag every night.

Final average score _3.14_ minus beginning average score _1.68_ = change _1.46_

Change _1.46_ divided by beginning score _1.68_ X 100 = percent change _86.9%_

You may also want to calculate the percent of responses to each question and compare those scores to analyze the change in each of the four response categories.

Post-Test Scores Reported as Percent

	Never	*Rarely*	*Often*	*Always*
I do my homework.	3	2	8	37
	6 percent	4 percent	16 percent	74 percent
I study for tests.	2	5	19	24
	4 percent	10 percent	38 percent	48 percent
I read every night.	4	6	10	30
	8 percent	12 percent	20 percent	60 percent
I organize my bookbag every night.	5	4	20	21
	10 percent	8 percent	40 percent	42 percent

Comparing Pre- and Post-Test Percent Scores

	Pre-Test	*Post-Test*
I do my homework.		
Never	40 percent	6 percent
Rarely	34 percent	4 percent
Often	12 percent	16 percent
Always	14 percent	74 percent

I study for tests.

Never	50 percent	4 percent
Rarely	28 percent	10 percent
Often	12 percent	38 percent
Always	14 percent	48 percent

I read every night.

Never	44 percent	8 percent
Rarely	22 percent	12 percent
Often	14 percent	20 percent
Always	20 percent	60 percent

I organize my bookbag every night.

Never	54 percent	10 percent
Rarely	28 percent	8 percent
Often	14 percent	40 percent
Always	4 percent	42 percent

By comparing percents for each response we can see the amount of growth in each category. Students have increased their confidence in their ability to perform these four study skill activities.

USING TECHNOLOGY TO AGGREGATE AND PRESENT YOUR DATA

Various tools are available to help with the process of aggregating data. If you use an electronic survey such as Survey Monkey, Google Docs, Naviance or Blackboard, data analysis tools available through these platforms offer various formats for analyzing and displaying your data. Tools such as EZanalyze (EZanalyze.com) also provide a way to import and analyze school data from the school's data system.

The Making DATA Work process offers simple paper and pencil procedures that rely on calculators, word processors and programs such as Excel. When using technology tools to organize and analyze your data it is important to understand the format that will best represent the data you have collected and will do the best job of helping you decide whether you have met your goal or answered the burning question.

Here are some technology links:

SchoolCounselor.com *for ppl. not good w/ @ technology*
www.schoolcounselor.com/
SchoolCounselor.com was created by Russell Sabella, Ph.D., for the purpose of advancing technology literacy among school counselors. This site contains links and updated information for his book, "SchoolCounselor.com: A Friendly and Practical Guide to the World Wide Web." Sabella publishes a free online newsletter focusing on technology issues, resources and activities and exploring free and almost free resources.

EZAnalyze *virus looking website*

www.ezanalyze.com/

EZAnalyze.com, developed by Tim Poynton, Ph.D., provides free, Excel-based tools designed to enhance the data-driven work of school counselors. EZanalyze is a Microsoft Excel Add-In for PCs that adds a "point and click" function for analyzing data and creating graphs. Time Tracker is a macro-enabled Excel workbook designed to perform note-keeping and time-tracking functions and generate reports for accountability and improved service to students.

Creating Surveys

Google Docs (forms) Sheets and Slides

Google Docs, Sheets and Slides are productivity apps that let you create different kinds of online documents, work on them in real time with other people and store them in your Google Drive online – all for free. You can access the documents, spreadsheets and presentations you create from any computer, anywhere in the world. (There's even some work you can do without an Internet connection.) This guide will give you a quick overview of the many things that you can do with Google Docs, Sheets and Slides.

http://support.google.com/drive/bin/answer.py?hl=en&answer=49008

Survey Monkey

www.surveymonkey.com/

Create and distribute surveys and analyze data for free for up to 10 questions and 100 participants. Many school districts have Survey Monkey accounts that permit users unlimited access to Survey Monkey resources.

Naviance *$ more for curriculum vs use @ home*

www.naviance.com/

Naviance is a college and career readiness platform that helps connect academic achievement to post-secondary goals.

Universal Encouragement Program

www.esi.cc

ESI's Universal Encouragement Program (UEP) helps states, districts and other groups of schools or education support programs assess and report student guidance needs, interests, experiences, progress and risk factors on a group-wide basis. The UEP shows program results across time. Using the UEP group-level data system you can:

- Provide custom assessments to schools and education support programs that are standardized for all group entities by customizing a UEP standard form or creating a new form
- Create group-level guidance reports
- Analyze impact of specific interventions in specific settings
- Deliver targeted communications to students and families via UEP school or program administrators

ANALYZING YOUR DATA

In summary, if you have developed your own survey you will need to turn the responses into a numeric value to analyze the data. If you have used a Likert scale then you can calculate an average response for each question. Below is a review of some basic statistical operations that will produce data you can analyze.

Calculating Averages (Mean Scores)

The average is the sum of the responses divided by the number of respondents.

FORMULA:

total score / number of participants = Average or Mean (X)

Example: 20 students responded to a question using a four-point Likert scale. Six chose never (1); five chose rarely (2); six chose often (3); and three chose always (4).
6 + 10 + 18 + 12 = 46 (total score)
46 / 20 = 2.3

Calculating Percents

Sometimes you will want to use percents. To calculate a percent, begin with a fraction (e.g., 20/100=20 percent). In other words, the part over the whole equals the percent. For example, if 325 out of 350 students graduate, then the graduation rate is 92 percent (325/350=92 percent).

FORMULA:

Part/Whole = N X 100 = percent

Example:
35 eighth-grade participants/70 eighth-graders = .50 X 100 = 50 percent

Calculating Percent of Change

Sometimes you will want to demonstrate the impact or the percent of change as a result of the intervention. When calculating percent of change follow the steps below.

FORMULA:

Final # (b) – beginning # (a) = change (c)
Change (c)/beginning # (a) X 100 = percent change
c/a = d x 100 = percent change

Example:
340 students graduate in 2013; 325 graduate in 2012.
340-325=15
15/325 X 100= 4.5 percent graduation rate increase from 2012 to 2013

Analyzing the data involves reviewing your results data to determine whether your goal has been met and/or what answers you have to the burning question. Consider the following questions:

- Did the intervention result in student growth in perception and/or outcome data?
- If the goal of the intervention was not met what changes are needed? Was the goal too high? Did the intervention address students' needs and the identified goal? Does the intervention need to be provided for a longer time period?
- What are the implications of the findings? Should the intervention be continued? Would more students benefit from this intervention?

SHARING YOUR RESULTS

OK, so you have your data. Now what do you do? Here is an example of how to take your data and put them in an easy-to-understand format to share with other stakeholders.

Pre-test and post-test of workshop using a five-point scale (1=strongly disagree, 2= disagree; 3=unsure; 4=agree; 5=strongly agree) and calculating the mean (average) responses by question:

	Pre-test	Post-test
Question 1	2.5	4.4
Question 2	2	4.8
Question 3	3	4.5

Put scores in Excel chart. (See Section IV for specific information about creating charts.)

Highlight the data, and select the chart-making function on your computer (e.g., Chart Wizard, Charts, Numbers or Google Forms) to make a chart from the data.

PRE- AND POST-TEST EXAMPLE

● Pre-Test   ● Post-Test

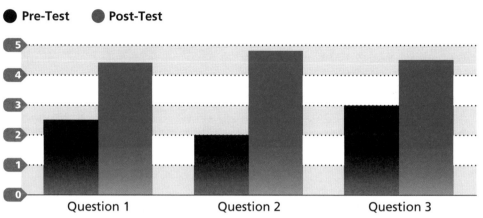

Compute the percent of change to determine impact.

Question 1
4.4 – 2.5 = 1.9   1.9/2.5 = 76 percent improvement in Question 1

Question 2
4.8 – 2 = 2.8   2.8/2 = 140 percent improvement in Question 2

Question 3
4.5 – 3 = 1.5   1.5/3 = 50 percent improvement in Question 3

Your next steps are to review your findings for program changes, and share your findings with stakeholders including teachers, administrators, parents, students and other school counselors.

Your Turn

Aggregate the following data, and answer the questions.

Twenty-five seniors register for a college preparation workshop consisting of four sessions. Before the workshop begins the 25 students complete the following survey using the following scale:

1=no, 2=unsure, 3=likely, 4=yes

I am planning to apply to a two- or four-year college.	1	2	3	4
I have identified three or more schools.	1	2	3	4
I know how to apply for financial aid or scholarships.	1	2	3	4
I know how to complete a college application.	1	2	3	4

Here is how the 25 students responded to each question *before* the workshop:

	No	Unsure	Likely	Yes
1. Planning on applying	3	6	12	4
2. Identified three or more schools	7	8	7	3
3. Financial aid/scholarship applications	10	9	5	1
4. Complete college application	15	5	3	2

Here is how the 25 students responded to each question after the workshop:

	No	Unsure	Likely	Yes
1. Planning on applying	0	1	3	21
2. Identified three or more schools	0	2	5	18
3. Financial aid/scholarship application	1	2	5	17
4. Complete college application	2	0	3	20

Calculate the pre- and post-test averages, or mean scores:

	Pre-test	Post-test
1. Planning on applying	2.68	3.92
2. Identified three or more schools	2.24	3.64
3. Financial aid/scholarship applications	1.88	3.52
4. Complete college application	1.68	3.64

Calculate the percent change for each question:

	Percent Change
1. Planning on applying	46.3%
2. Identified three or more schools	62.5%
3. Financial aid/scholarship applications	87.2%
4. Complete college application	116.7% ?

What does the percent change mean about each question?

Now calculate the percent of students that responded to each question according to the scale:

(Hint: if four students answered yes to question one, that would be 16 percent of the students.)

	No	Unsure	Likely	Yes
1. Planning on applying	12	24	48	16
2. Identified three or more schools	28	32	28	12
3. Financial aid/scholarship applications	40	36	20	4
4. Complete college application	60	20	12	8

Here is how the 25 students responded to each question *after* the workshop:

	No	Unsure	Likely	Yes
1. Planning on applying	0	4	12	84
2. Identified three or more schools	0	8	20	72
3. Financial aid/scholarship applications	4	8	20	68
4. Complete college application	8	0	12	80

Based on your analysis of the data what is your assessment about the success of your intervention? Was your goal met?

-Book doesn't say what the goal was
- Does a significantly great job at incr.
   student awareness of college where 84% are
   now planning on applying vs. 16%

ANALYZING QUALITATIVE DATA

Analyzing qualitative data is a legitimate way to understand educational issues. Students' stories can characterize an issue in useful ways. Qualitative data can be gathered in a variety of ways: open-ended questions included on a survey, interview data and focus groups.

Qualitative data are a powerful way to understand a group's perspective and can shed light on the meaning of quantitative data. In other words, you may know that 40 percent of your ninth-graders have one or more failing grade, but you may not know why they are failing. Asking students what interferes with their academic progress and what might help is a way to understand the issue. Qualitative data can be useful when developing intervention strategies.

Here are some suggestions for organizing, aggregating and analyzing qualitative data. This is a basic version of coding.

- Transcribe the qualitative data (copy responses to open-ended questions on surveys to a new document, or transcribe a recording of the focus group or interview).
- Code the data according to large groupings or categories. The categories may be based on an *a priori* coding scheme (codes are known or agreed upon before the coding process begins) or an open coding scheme (where you group similar responses and give the group of responses a name that represents the group).
- Summarize or name each large category of data.
- Reporting these large groupings or categories can be powerful. Count up the number of responses that convey the same thing, and report that number too. For example, "Ten students (out of 30) say the first time they were bullied was in elementary school." Reporting the number of students (or translating it to a percent) is a powerful statement about the depth of the bullying problem.
- It may be that you want to look more deeply into these large groups of data. Follow the same procedure. Organize responses within the large group so similar responses are together. For instance it may be that five of the elementary bullying stories were about being bullied on the school bus. You can report, "Five of the 30 students reported being bullied on the school bus when they were in elementary school."

Organizing Qualitative Data

On the left are 21 student responses to the question: What is one thing the school could do that would increase attendance?" On the right these 21 responses have been organized into groups, or categories. These qualitative data on first review appear to fit into four groups: time-related issues, educational issues, getting help/fairness from teachers and bullying. These data can be reported in several ways. For example it could be reported that four out of 21 made suggestions concerning time factors (18 percent), or seven students out of 21 were concerned about educational issues such as homework and school instruction (33 percent). When looking at these data Manager Middle School may be surprised to see how many student responses are about the quality of their education and teacher treatment.

Student responses:
- School should start later.
- No homework.
- Make teachers be fair.
- I don't know.
- Make the bullies stop.
- Tell Mrs. Jones to stop being mean.
- Homework shouldn't count.
- Make school more fun.
- Let us come in late.
- Most teacher-created strategies don't work.
- Stop calling me names (bad), hurting me, embarrassing me.
- Homework should only be due on Mondays.
- Change the time school starts.
- Make math more fun.
- Help me with my school work.
- Give me a computer at home.
- Change the rules about attendance.
- Tell the patrols on the bus to do their job.
- Get Andre to leave everyone alone.
- Make lunch time longer.
- Tell the teachers to make their subjects more interesting.

Time-Related Issues:
- School should start later.
- Let us come in late.
- Change the time school starts.
- Make lunch time longer.

Educational Issues:
- No homework.
- Homework shouldn't count.
- Make school more fun.
- Homework should only be due on Mondays.
- Tell the teachers to make their subjects more interesting.
- Make math more fun.
- Give me a computer at home.

Getting Help/Fairness From Teachers
- Most teacher-created strategies don't work.
- Make teachers be fair.
- Tell Mrs. Jones to stop being mean.
- Help me with my school work.

Bullying
- Make the bullies stop.
- Stop calling me names (bad), hurting me, embarrassing me.
- Tell the patrols on the bus to do their job.
- Get Andre to leave everyone alone.

Other
- Change the rules about attendance.
- I don't know.

EXAMPLES OF TRACK

TRACK EXAMPLE 1:

Somewhere Elementary School
Track: How will you analyze the data?

Demographic data helps school counselors understand the target population. Analysis of the perception data, the student surveys, will show where students think their problems are and why they think they have problems. Analysis of the faculty surveys will show if faculty perceptions align with the students' perceptions.

Findings will be reported in Excel graph and chart form.

FACULTY SURVEY RESPONSES:

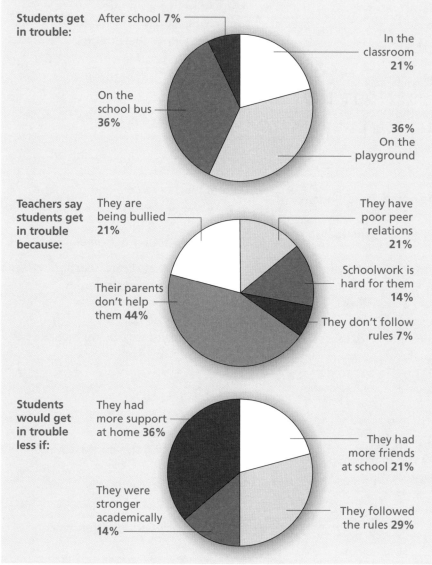

Students get in trouble:
- After school **7%**
- In the classroom **21%**
- On the school bus **36%**
- **36%** On the playground

Teachers say students get in trouble because:
- They are being bullied **21%**
- They have poor peer relations **21%**
- Schoolwork is hard for them **14%**
- Their parents don't help them **44%**
- They don't follow rules **7%**

Students would get in trouble less if:
- They had more support at home **36%**
- They had more friends at school **21%**
- They were stronger academically **14%**
- They followed the rules **29%**

STUDENT SURVEY RESPONSES:

Students say they have the most trouble following rules:

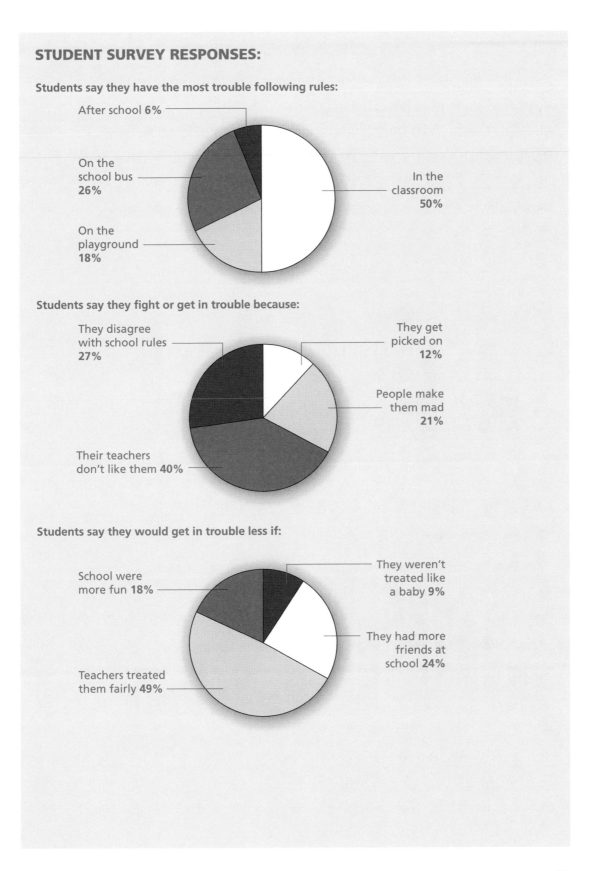

After school **6%**

On the school bus **26%**

On the playground **18%**

In the classroom **50%**

Students say they fight or get in trouble because:

They disagree with school rules **27%**

They get picked on **12%**

People make them mad **21%**

Their teachers don't like them **40%**

Students say they would get in trouble less if:

School were more fun **18%**

They weren't treated like a baby **9%**

They had more friends at school **24%**

Teachers treated them fairly **49%**

Track: How will you make sense of the data?

Summarize the results, and use graphs and charts to capture key findings.

Number of students in group: eight (all male)

Number of behavioral referrals before intervention: 24 (August–January)

Number of behavioral referrals after intervention: Nine (January–June)

PRE- AND POST-TEST SCORES FROM SURVEY ADMINISTERED BEFORE AND AFTER PARTICIPATING IN GROUP COUNSELING:

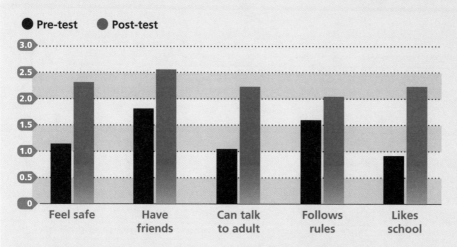

GRADES BEFORE AND AFTER GROUP COUNSELING

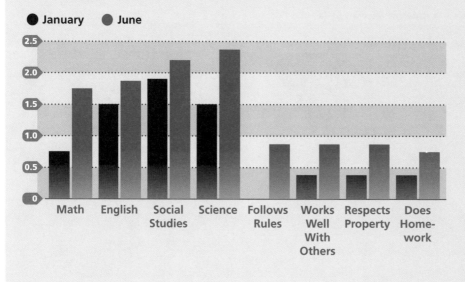

Mistry Middle School

Track: How will you analyze the data?

Demographic data will help the school counselors understand the target population. How many of these students are English-language learners, have an IEP, have previously earned low/failing grades, etc. Being able to identify the characteristics of this group and look for commonalities may be useful for developing remediation strategies.

Analysis of the data from the survey will help school counselors, teachers and administrators understand school failure from the student perspective. This information will also be useful when considering remediation strategies.

Findings will be reported in Excel graph and chart form, and all responses to the question "One thing that would help me" will be shared.

Demographic data

- 50 identified students with D/F grades at first interim
- 40 percent of the students (20) are eighth-graders; 60 percent (30) are seventh-graders
- 80 percent (40) are male; 30 percent (15) are English-language learners; 15 percent (seven) have an IEP; 60 percent (30) are on free/reduced lunch
- 50 percent (25) are African-American; 30 percent (15) are Hispanic; and 20 percent (10) white

Survey findings:

- 50 percent of students do not feel the staff help them improve grades (never or seldom).
- 70 percent of students say post-secondary education is important to them (usually or always).
- 60 percent of students say they don't have an adult to talk to (never or seldom).
- 76 percent of students report they don't stay after school for help.
- Some of the responses to the question "One thing that would help me…":
  Teachers should treat me nicer.
  Teachers need to talk slower and explain things more than once.
  Having help from an older student would help me.
  I could do better if there weren't so many bullies at this school.

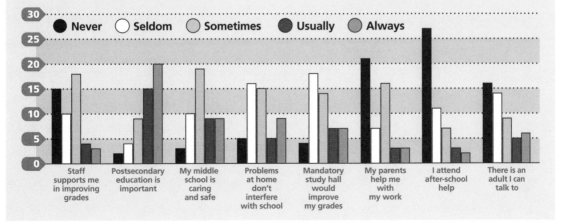

Anywhere High School

Track: How will you analyze the data?

Summarize the results, and use graphs and charts to capture key findings.

Data analysis from the survey will help school counselors, teachers and administrators understand enrollment barriers and retention issues. School counselors anticipate significant impact statements will result from investigation of this question.

Survey Results

Some of the 10th-grade findings are:

- 70 percent of the students who enrolled in high school courses in eighth grade were more likely to enroll and complete honors courses than students who didn't enroll in high school credit courses in eighth grade.
- 65 percent of the students didn't correlate course rigor with post-secondary options.
- 45 percent of the minority students indicated they were never encouraged to enroll in rigorous courses.
- 50 percent of students enrolled in a rigorous course were embarrassed to ask questions during class.
- 25 percent of students reported that language barriers prohibited their parents from understanding the academic advisement process.

School Counselor Supervisor Achievement High School

Track: How will you make sense of the data?

Summarize the results, and use graphs and charts to capture key findings.

Analyzing student enrollment patterns, pre- and post-test results, attendance data, club participation and behavioral referrals will provide quantitative feedback. The focus group is intended to provide qualitative feedback and give additional voice to the data. Both methods are intended to measure the impact of new student transitioning and program effectiveness. A few key quantitative and qualitative findings are:

Quantitative analysis:
- 100 new students participated in the new student orientation program.
- Attendance records indicate that none (0 percent) of the new students had more than three unexcused absences.
- 90 percent of the 100 students were earning passing grades.
- 5 percent of the 100 students earned behavioral infractions requiring out-of-school suspension. Although all five students were passing their classes, they did not participate in a club or after-school activity.
- 45 percent of the 100 students participated in clubs or after-school activities.

Qualitative analysis:
- Students who participated in a club or after-school activity reported having at least five friends.
- Students who participated in a club or after-school activity reported high school spirit.
- Students who had behavioral referrals didn't report participating in clubs or after-school activities.
- After-school commitments such as work and lack of transportation prevented some students from participating.
- Students would prefer to have mentors who are the same grade level.
- Students would like more activities involving their mentors.
- Students would like for their mentors to provide academic tutoring or a referral list of tutors.

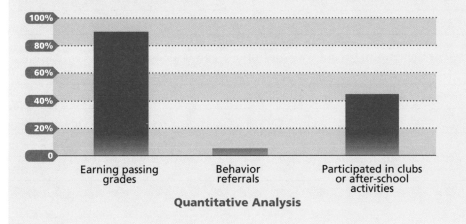

Quantitative Analysis

TRACK WORKSHEET

How can you aggregate, collate or disaggregate the data to determine whether you have achieved your goal?

_____

_____

_____

_____

_____

Are you reporting process, perception and outcome data?

_____

_____

_____

_____

_____

How can you use technology to support the process?

_____

_____

_____

_____

_____

What can you learn from analyzing the data?

_____

_____

_____

_____

_____

How can you present the data in such a way that others can understand it?

_____

_____

_____

_____

_____

PART IV

Announce: How Will You Share Your Results?

Keys to Using Your Results

- What do the results mean?
- How will you use the results?
- What are the implications of your results?
- What are the recommendations?
- With whom will you share the results?

Once you have collected and analyzed the data it is time to consider what the data mean for your students and your program. After analyzing the data you will want to consider how you will you use your data and how you will share your findings with others. Sharing data with stakeholders can lead to increased support of school counseling programs and earning the respect of administrators, teachers and parents. Share data reports at faculty meetings, team meetings, leadership meetings, in PTA newsletters and on bulletin boards in the building.

This final step, sharing the data, is critical to fostering relationships and demonstrating the impact on closing achievement gaps and enhancing student success. Helping stakeholders understand educational issues not only benefits students but the process contributes to stakeholders' appreciation for the role of school counselors as data-driven decision makers.

What do the results mean?

First, consider what you learned from the data and how to use these results and recommendations. Will you use the information to modify or improve existing programs? Advocate for new programs? Demonstrate effectiveness of existing programs? Have you met your school counseling program goal? What are the implications from the data about the goal or the intervention? Do the data answer the burning question?

How will you use the data?

Use the data to:

- Improve, modify or change services provided to students
- Eliminate programs or services that are not meeting intended needs
- Create new programs
- Evaluate existing programs
- Demonstrate school counselor effectiveness

What are the implications of the data?

Before making recommendations consider the implications.

Implications from the data may indicate that increasing school counseling services to address a particular need is warranted. Or that group interventions have more of an impact on student learning than classroom lessons for reducing test-taking anxiety. An implication may be that more data are needed. Perhaps collecting perception data from parents will shed new light on an attendance issue. Implications sometimes result in making recommendations.

What are the recommendations?

Recommendations are those specific steps that school counselors, administrators or stakeholders should consider. Recommendations infer action.

Examples of recommendations:

- Share data with administrators, and consider modifying the tardy policy.
- Increase small group counseling for at-risk ninth-grade students.
- Modify the after-school tutoring program to accommodate the late bus schedule.

SHARING THE RESULTS

With whom will you share your results?

Once you've collected the data, disaggregated or organized it in some meaningful way and have considered the implications and recommendations, it is important to begin planning how you'll use the data and how you'll share the results with stakeholders. The power of data is sharing results with others.

How will you present your results?

Another important consideration is how to present your results. Administrators, teachers and parents are more likely to be engaged with the results if they are presented in a one-page format. Consider using a one-page report that briefly offers the reason data were collected (the goal or the question); the data-collection strategies; the results reported in bullet, chart or graph format; and the recommendations or implications of the data. Using Microsoft Excel, you can easily convert data into a graph or chart using the Chart function of your computer.

USING THE DATA REPORT FORM

You can use the DATA report form to share results with stakeholders. The report form provides a brief review of the purpose of the data-gathering project, the methods used to examine or collect data, the results and the implications or recommendations that can be made based on the results. More information can be provided to the stakeholders but the DATA Report Form provides an overview.

Formatting the DATA report form (using Microsoft Office 2010 for PC):

1. Open a new document. Use Arial Unicode MS 12 font; bold and centered for headings. Use Arial Narrow MS 11 or 10 for text.
2. On the first line type **School Counseling Program DATA Report** (Arial Unicode MS 12 font; bold and centered).
3. On second line type the name of the school, the date and possibly the reporting school counselor's name (bold and centered). Enter to go to the next line.
4. Click Insert and open Table and click on Insert Table. When the Insert Table chart pops up ask for two columns and four rows. Click Okay.
5. Put your cursor on the line forming the columns and drag to the left so the first column is approximately half-inch wide. Using your cursor on the row lines move them down to open the size of the rows.
6. Using your cursor highlight the first column. With column highlighted go to Layout and choose Text Direction. Choose the direction that is centered and facing left. You may have to click the Text Direction icon to get the text going in the desired direction. Type the words in bold and caps: DESIGN, ASK, TRACK and ANNOUNCE.
7. With the column still highlighted choose Design and Shading. Pick the color you would like to use for the headings and select.
8. Now you are ready to input the information below. By putting your cursor on the row line you can move the line up and down to accommodate the space you need for each section. Work toward fitting everything into one page.

Formatting the DATA Report form
(using Microsoft Word for Macintosh):

1. Open a new document. Use Arial Unicode MS 12 font; bold and centered for headings. Use Arial Narrow MS 11 or 10 for text.
2. On the first line type **School Counseling Program DATA Report**.
3. On second line type the name of the school, the date and possibly the reporting school counselor's name (bold and centered). Enter to go to the next line.
4. Click Table tab. Choose Insert. Click Table. When the Insert Table chart pops up ask for two columns and four rows. Click Okay.
5. Put your cursor on the line that forms the columns and drag to the left so that the first column is approximately half-inch wide. Using your cursor on the row lines move them down to open the size of the rows.
6. Using your cursor highlight the first column. With column highlighted go to Format and choose Text Direction. Choose the direction that is centered and facing left. Type the words in bold and caps: DESIGN, ASK, TRACK and ANNOUNCE.
7. Highlight the column and open Formatting Palette. Choose Borders and Shading. Pick the color you would like to use for the headings and select.
8. Now you are ready to input the information below. By putting your cursor on the row line you can move the line up and down to accommodate the space you need for each section. Work toward fitting everything into one page.

COMPLETE THE FOUR-STEP DATA REPORT FORM:

DESIGN

Briefly (one-two sentences) explain the purpose of the data-gathering project. State the SMART goal or research question.

ASK

Provide a brief description of the procedures. List the questions (or some of the questions) from any survey you created to collect perception data.

TRACK

Provide the results. Use charts and descriptive statements to summarize the results. Report process, perception and outcome data. Copy charts from Excel data and fit to TRACK box. If you collected qualitative data summarize briefly and/or provide representative statements.

ANNOUNCE

With whom will you share these data? Consider the audience when reporting recommendations and implications. List the implications resulting from the data as well as recommendations or next steps.

Create a one-page DATA report form following the directions on page 77 for PC and page 78 for Mac. Choose one of the school examples found at the end of each chapter (Design, Ask, Track, Announce). Practice putting the required information into each of the four boxes. Consider, what information the stakeholder needs to have to understand how and why you chose the goal or question, how you collected and analyzed the data and the resulting implications and recommendations.

Here are the page numbers to find the information about each school example:

Somewhere Elementary School

Mistry Middle School

Anywhere High School

Example DATA reports for these three schools can be found on page sthe following pages:

SCHOOL COUNSELING PROGRAM DATA REPORT

Name of School: _____ Date: _____

DESIGN	State your program goal or research question and purpose.
ASK	Describe the data-collection strategies.
TRACK	Summarize the results, and use graphs and charts to capture key results.
ANNOUNCE	Describe the implications and recommendations to stakeholders.

ANNOUNCE EXAMPLES

The following examples describe the implications/recommendations and how the results will be shared with the stakeholders.

ANNOUNCE EXAMPLE 1:

Somewhere Elementary School
Announce: How will you share your results?

Implications:
- Student and teacher perceptions of the cause of misbehavior are different.
- Student perception data were used to develop the intervention.
- Group counseling was an effective intervention. Discipline referrals are down, and grades and behavioral marks improved.
- Connecting with students improves behavior and grades.

Recommendations:
- Share data with faculty and administration. Discuss the different perceptions of students and teachers.
- Get input from teachers about next steps.
- Consider using more group counseling for identified students; conduct further investigation of school climate.

[See pages 110-111 for the Somewhere Elementary DATA report example.]

ANNOUNCE EXAMPLE 2:

Mistry Middle School
Announce: How will you share your results?

- The school counseling team will review demographic and survey data and share results with the administration, advisory council and teachers.
- Decisions about remediation strategies will be made in collaboration with faculty and administration.

Recommendations:
- After reviewing the data it may be necessary to gather additional information using a school climate survey for all students in the school or a bullying behavior survey.
- Students may benefit from small-group counseling focusing on school success strategies and goal setting.
- Teachers may benefit from workshops focusing on working with diverse students (English-language learners, IEP, students of color).

[See pages 116-117 for the Mistry Middle School DATA report example.]

Anywhere High School
Announce: How will you share your results?

The school counseling team will review demographic data and survey results and share them with administrators and teachers. Decisions about enrollment patterns and retention strategies will be made in collaboration with faculty and administration.

Recommendations:
- Schedule middle and high school counselor/administrator collaboration meetings to discuss vertical academic/career counseling strategies.
- Create a schoolwide mentoring culture encouraging college readiness and preparation.
- Share results of the survey with school staff; explore strategies to increase student participation and self-efficacy.
- Translate all materials intended for parental action into multiple languages, and distribute multiple ways.

[See pages 120-121 for the Anywhere High School DATA Report Example.]

School Counselor Supervisor Achievement High School
Announce: How will you share your results?

All data will be compiled and presented at the end-of-year retreat. Additionally, data will be shared with the administration, advisory council and new students who participated in the program.

Possible Recommendations:
- Pair mentors and new students by grade level.
- Recruit additional mentors.
- Inform students about possible tutorial services.
- Seek to eliminate barriers prohibiting students from participating in a club or after-school activity.
- Provide equitable services for new students who are struggling academically or have behavioral referrals.

ANNOUNCE WORKSHEET

What do these results mean?

_____

_____

_____

_____

_____

How will you use the results?

_____

_____

_____

_____

_____

What are the implications of your results?

_____

_____

_____

_____

_____

What are the recommendations?

_____

_____

_____

_____

_____

With whom will you share the results?

_____

_____

_____

_____

_____

PART V

Examples

Examples of the Four-Step Making DATA Work Process

MANAGER MIDDLE SCHOOL EXAMPLE

Here is an example of how one school applied the Making DATA Work process.

MANAGER MIDDLE SCHOOL MISSION STATEMENT:

Manager Middle School is committed to providing academic excellence in a safe, positive environment in which diversity is respected and all students feel invited and expected to become participants in their own academic, career, personal and social growth.

After reviewing the school's data (see the data review in Design, pp. 23), the school counselors were concerned that the decrease in attendance and increase in safety offenses were a result of the transition of many new students to the school. Were the attendance and safety issues related to a lack of student engagement? Were teachers responding to new students' needs? What did the students think about Manager Middle School? And what about the parents' views? The school counselors decided to focus on understanding the attendance issue before implementing an intervention.

Design Worksheet Example:

What is the gap, issue or student need you are addressing?
It has come to the attention of the school counselors at Manager Middle School that in spite of a variety of activities aimed at increasing student attendance Manager Middle School's attendance rate for the previous year dropped to 89 percent. Manager Middle School is in a suburban area with a diverse school population, and approximately 30 percent of students are economically disadvantaged. The school counselors and administrators are interested in increasing attendance. To achieve this goal they want to understand the perception of students and parents concerning the factors contributing to poor attendance before implementing a program.

How does addressing the issue affect student achievement?

The school counselors and administrators know a poor attendance rate affects achievement and participation in school activities. They are also aware of the relationship between lack of success in middle school and dropping out in high school. Although they have tried the traditional responses to absenteeism such as calls home, letters to parents and reports to truant officers, the rate has actually increased, not decreased. The school counselors have decided a systemic approach is in order. Before implementing new strategies they will collect perception data from students and parents.

Is there a burning question that should be answered before identifying the goal?

After reviewing the school data, the school improvement plan and the current school counseling services used to address the attendance issue the school counselors realize they need more information about the cause of the decrease in attendance. They decide to collect perception data from students and parents to understand the attendance issue.

The burning question:

What are the factors contributing to poor attendance at Manager Middle School?

Is the goal based on existing data?

The school counselors suspect school attendance is influenced by a variety of factors currently not understood by faculty and administration. Although the school has made adequate yearly progress every year some concerns have not been adequately addressed, and an achievement gap still exists at Manager Middle School. The increase in absenteeism and increase in safety issues are of concern to the school counselors. They suspect addressing these issues will ultimately have an impact on student achievement.

How does your goal align with the school's mission statement or school improvement plan?

The school's mission statement states Manager Middle School is "committed to providing academic excellence in a safe, positive environment in which diversity is respected, and all students feel invited and expected to become participants in their own academic, career, personal and social growth." Manager Middle School has also identified a school improvement plan item stating Manager Middle School will "sustain a school climate supporting student achievement through the promotion of positive student participation in school." Both the mission statement and the school improvement plan are based on the premise that attending school regularly is an important component to academic achievement, school success and staying in school.

What is your school counseling program goal?

School attendance will increase from the previous school year from 89 percent to 91 percent by school year-end.

Ask Worksheet Example

What data do you need to develop your SMART goal plan?

Recognizing the impact attendance has on academic achievement, the school counselors seek to determine the factors contributing to increased absenteeism at their middle school. For example, determining who the students are by ethnicity, gender and grade level would be critical data elements to evaluate. The perceptions of the students, teachers and parents concerning high absences are also factors to explore.

Do the data exist, and are they available?

To understand the issue and meet the goal, school counselors reviewed attendance data in the student information system to determine who has eight or more absences and will disaggregate the group according to demographic factors. Perception data about the issue will be collected from students and parents.

Identified population

Students identified with eight or more absences (n=130) will be invited to complete a survey. Parents of the 130 students will also be asked to complete a survey.

What are your action steps? What formal and informal approvals do you need?

The school counselors informed administrators of their intentions and gained approval to determine the factors contributing to poor attendance. Next, they initiated and convened a meeting with stakeholders to discuss the issue. The invited stakeholders consisted of all school counselors, a teacher and administrative representative, the school psychologist, the truancy office and the student government president.

Do you need to create data-collection instruments?

After collaborating with stakeholders and listening to recommendations, the school counselors developed a one-page survey to gain student and ultimately parental input. The survey consisted of five questions.

What is your timeline for planning data collection, analyzing and sharing the data?

The school counselors decided to engage the cooperation of the truancy officer to assist with survey administration. Data-collection strategies began immediately and concluded within 30 days of the survey through a variety of techniques: hard copy, electronically and postal mail. Next, the school counselors aggregated the data within a two-week timeframe.

SCHOOL SUCCESS SURVEY ~ ATTENDANCE

Manager Middle School

Dear Parents,
The faculty of Manager Middle School want to understand barriers to student attendance. Would you help us by completing the following survey? Please circle a number from 1 to 5 for each statement.

1. I believe the staff (teachers, school counselors, assistant principals) at Manager Middle School support my son/daughter in improving his/her grades.

   1-Never   2-Seldom   3-Sometimes   4-Usually   5-Always

2. I believe it is important for my son/daughter to go to college or get further education after high school.

   1-Never   2-Seldom   3-Sometimes   4-Usually   5-Always

3. My son/daughter's school is a safe place.

   1-Never   2-Seldom   3-Sometimes   4-Usually   5-Always

4. I believe it is important for my son/daughter to attend school every day.

   1-Never   2-Seldom   3-Sometimes   4-Usually   5-Always

5. I help my son/daughter at home with school work.

   1-Never   2-Seldom   3-Sometimes   4-Usually   5-Always

6. My son/daughter has been teased/bullied at school.

   Yes   No

7 My child misses school for the following reasons:

   _____ Sickness   _____ Does not have homework completed

   _____ Overslept   Other: _____

   _____ Being bullied

What is one thing the school could do that would increase school attendance?

_____

_____

_____

_____

SCHOOL SUCCESS SURVEY ~ ATTENDANCE

Manager Middle School

Dear Students,

The faculty of Manager Middle School want to understand reasons for student absences. Would you help us by completing the following survey? Please circle a number from 1 to 5 for each statement.

1. I believe the staff (teachers, school counselors, assistant principals) at Manager Middle School help me improve my grades.

   1-Never   2-Seldom   3-Sometimes   4-Usually   5-Always

2. I believe it is important for me to go to college or get further education after high school.

   1-Never   2-Seldom   3-Sometimes   4-Usually   5-Always

3. I believe Manager Middle School is a safe place.

   1-Never   2-Seldom   3-Sometimes   4-Usually   5-Always

4. I believe it is important to attend school every day.

   1-Never   2-Seldom   3-Sometimes   4-Usually   5-Always

5. I like to come to school.

   1-Never   2-Seldom   3-Sometimes   4-Usually   5-Always

6. Have you been bullied at Manager Middle School?

   Yes   No

7. I miss school for the following reasons:

   _____ I am sick.   _____ I don't like school.

   _____ I oversleep and miss the bus.   _____ I haven't done my homework.

   _____ I am being bullied.   Other: _____

What is one thing the school could do that would increase school attendance?

_____

_____

_____

_____

What are the factors contributing to poor school attendance at Manager Middle School?

Target population: Students attending Manager Middle School

Random sample: All students with three or more absences and equal chance of selection

Purposive sample: Students with three or more absences in ninth grade

Convenient sample: Student with three or more absences and available to complete the survey

Track Worksheet Example

How can you aggregate, collate or disaggregate the data to determine whether you have achieved your goal?

The data will be used to help school counselors and administrators understand the depth and nature of the attendance problem at Manager Middle School. The student data will help to answer the question: What are the factors contributing to low school attendance at Manager Middle School? The student data will also provide some students' comments about their reasons for not attending school. The parent data will help the school counselors and administrators understand the parent perspective of the attendance issue. Specifically, the school counselors are interested in hearing whether students and parents at Manager Middle School think it's a safe school and that there are adults that will help. They are also looking for information about the student and parent beliefs about education.

What do you learn from analyzing the data?

The data will be aggregated according to response categories (student and parent survey data: never-sometimes-always). Average scores will be obtained for each of the five Likert-scale questions. Both students and parents will also be asked to indicate all the reasons school is missed. These data will be reported in the aggregate. A final open-ended question will ask what suggestions parents and students can offer.

How can you present the data so others can understand it?

Providing the student and parent data in chart form will allow for comparison of the data. A pie chart will be used to report reasons for absences. And, finally, open-ended responses to the question about what suggestions participants have for increasing attendance will be organized into categories of like meaning.

Are you presenting process, perception and outcome data?

The data will be presented in a one-page data report form. Charts will be used to summarize the student and parent responses to the survey.

Announce Worksheet Example

What do these results mean?

One hundred thirty students completed the survey. Results indicate that minority students have the highest absentee rate. A significant number of the student respondents believe attending school is seldom–sometimes important. In contrast, a significant number of parents indicate that attending school is sometimes–usually important.

Considerations will be given to determine why minority students have the highest absentee rate. We will also examine the relationship between absences and GPA and review systemic interventions to address the issue of absentees.

How will you use the results?

Implications suggest students with poor attendance do not connect attendance with academic achievement, do not participate in school clubs or athletic activities and engage in limited social activities when attending school.

Parental responses indicate a significant number of parents experienced negative school encounters that ultimately led to dropping out of school or completing high school later in life.

With whom will you share the results?

Results will be shared with all stakeholders (administration, faculty, parents, teachers, students) invested in why attendance is poor at Manager Middle School.

What are the implications of your findings?

Findings will be presented in a DATA report using pie charts to report responses to factors contributing to poor attendance at Manager Middle School.

What are the recommendations?

Findings will be used to develop interventions and aggressively target student populations with high truancy and absenteeism. School and outreach parent workshops will commence for the remainder of the school year.

Manager Middle School DATA Report

D ESIGN

Purpose: Manager Middle School is in an urban area with 30 percent economically disadvantaged students. End-of-year attendance reports indicate the attendance rate at Manager Middle School is 89 percent. The school counselors and administrators are interested in increasing attendance by understanding the factors contributing to poor attendance before implementing a program.

Goal: To increase attendance from 89 percent in the previous year to 91 percent by school year-end.

A SK

The following procedures were used to investigate this issue:

■ School attendance records were examined, and all students with eight or more absences complete a survey. The survey consists of five questions (e.g. The staff supports me; school is important; I like school, etc.) using a five-point Likert scale (never-seldom-sometimes-usually-always), with one question about being bullied and one open-ended question (what can the school do to increase attendance?)

■ Demographic information about this group was disaggregated.

■ A similar survey was sent to parents of the identified group of students.

■ Intervention to increase attendance will be implemented based on perception data findings.

T RACK

Demographic findings: Of the 130 students with eight or more absences, economically disadvantaged students account for 48 percent of the absences.

Students: (130 identified students completed the survey). Students believe attending school is seldom-sometimes (2.3) important and that Manager Middle School is seldom (2) safe; 73 (56 percent) students say they are bullied.

Parents: (65/130 parents returned the survey). Parents say attending school is important sometimes-usually (3.2) and they never-seldom (1.6) help with homework; 40 (62 percent) say that their child is bullied.

STUDENT RESPONSES

- Teachers help me improve my grades
- It is important for me to go to college
- Manager Middle School is a safe place
- It is important to attend school
- I like to come to school

PARENT RESPONSES

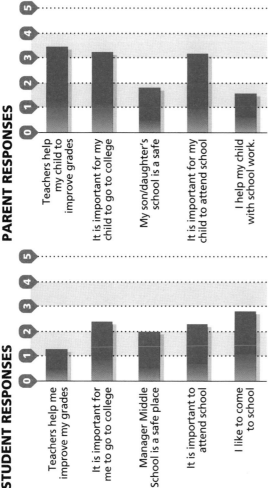

- Teachers help my child to improve grades
- It is important for my child to go to college
- My son/daughter's school is a safe
- It is important for my child to attend school
- I help my child with school work.

A NNOUNCE

Summary: Students and parents report being bullied and not feeling safe at school as primary reasons for absences.

Implications/Recommendations:

- Share findings with administration and faculty; consider implications of findings and get faculty input.
- Consider what findings about bullying, feeling safe and liking school mean for the school.
- Look at demographic data to consider why Hispanic students have the highest absentee rate followed by African-Americans.
- Look at the relationship between absences and GPA.
- Consider systemic change responses to address this issue.
- Consider parent and student suggestions (open-ended questions) about increasing attendance.
- Consider how offering parent workshops, group counseling, classroom lessons might address the issue.

Survey Examples

FIFTH-GRADE PEER MEDIATOR TRAINING SURVEY

Please complete the following survey. Circle the number that best describes you.

1 *Strongly Disagree/ Never*	2 *Disagree/ Not Very Often*	3 *Not Sure/ Sometimes*	4 *Agree/ Most of the time*	5 *Strongly Agree/ Always*

	1	2	3	4	5
1. I feel good about myself.	1	2	3	4	5
2. I can work out problems with friends.	1	2	3	4	5
3. I am able to deal with stress.	1	2	3	4	5
4. I can say what I am thinking and feeling to others.	1	2	3	4	5
5. I can solve my own problems with friends.	1	2	3	4	5
6. I can help others solve problems.	1	2	3	4	5
7. I know how to make and keep friends.	1	2	3	4	5

ELEMENTARY SMALL-GROUP COUNSELING EVALUATION

Study Group Post-Group Survey

Please answer the following questions as honestly as possible. Your answers will be anonymous, so please do not write your name on this survey. The answers that you provide will give me information to see if this group was helpful. Thank you.

Mark all that apply – Check the box

1. Which subjects are the most difficult for you?
   - ☐ Reading
   - ☐ Writing
   - ☐ Math
   - ☐ Social studies
   - ☐ Science

2. What do you think makes it difficult for you to do well on tests?
   - ☐ The information
   - ☐ Not enough time
   - ☐ Nervous
   - ☐ Tired
   - ☐ Remembering the important information
   - ☐ Got confused by the test question
   - Other_____

3. Which study strategies do you use when you study?
   - ☐ Note reviews
   - ☐ Quiz myself
   - ☐ Quizzed by others
   - ☐ Flashcards
   - ☐ Practice questions
   - ☐ Study groups
   - ☐ Read and listen
   - ☐ Relaxation strategies
   - ☐ Quick thinkers
   - ☐ Beat the clock
   - Other_____

Turn Over

4. How do you use your agenda?

☐ Write down assignments

☐ Track when I complete assignments

☐ List the materials I need to complete assignments

☐ Plan for long-term projects

Mark only one answer choice – Circle the number

5. Since beginning this study group, when do you study?

   1) Never

   2) Only before state tests

   3) Only before a test

   4) Every week

   5) Every night

6. Since beginning this study group, approximately how much time do you spend studying (not counting completing homework) per week?

   1) 0-1 hours per week

   2) 2-3 hours per week

   3) 4-5 hours per week

   4) 6-7 hours per week

   5) 8 or more hours per week

7. Since beginning this study group, how prepared do you normally feel when you take a test?

   1) Not prepared at all

   2) Only a little bit prepared

   3) Somewhat prepared

   4) Prepared

   5) Very prepared

Created by Sofia Echaide-Viafara, 2012

ELEMENTARY SURVEY

Closing the Science Gap 2012

For each question, circle the answer that best describes you:

1. I like to learn about nature.

   1-No   2-Not really   3-A little   4-Yes

2. I think girls are just as good as boys at things like math and science.

   1-No   2-Not really   3-A little   4-Yes

3. I know how to study.

   1-No   2-Not really   3-A little   4-Yes

4. If I try hard, I usually succeed.

   1-No   2-Not really   3-A little   4-Yes

5. I think experiments are interesting and fun.

   1-No   2-Not really   3-A little   4-Yes

6. I have good test-taking skills.

   1-No   2-Not really   3-A little   4-Yes

7. I think boys are better at math and science than girls are.

   1-No   2-Not really   3-A little   4-Yes

8. I am organized and can always find things in my desk or backpack.

   1-No   2-Not really   3-A little   4-Yes

9. I am a smart person.

   1-No   2-Not really   3-A little   4-Yes

10. I do my homework every night.

    1-No   2-Not really   3-A little   4-Yes

My grade _____ My teacher _____

One thing I think would help me do better in science is:

_____

_____

Created by Kris Griswold, 2012

DISCIPLINE REFERRALS SURVEY
AT SOMEWHERE ELEMENTARY SCHOOL

Dear Teachers,

Please complete this anonymous questionnaire to help the school counselor and administrator understand the discipline issues at our school. Respond by rating your top three answers with a 1, 2, 3:

Students at Somewhere Elementary School get in trouble:

    In the classroom   _____

    On the playground   _____

    On the school bus   _____

    After school   _____

    None of these   _____

    Other_____

The reason students fight or get in trouble is because:

    They are being bullied.   _____

    They have poor peer relations.   _____

    School work is hard for them.   _____

    They don't follow the rules.   _____

    Their parents don't help them.   _____

    None of these   _____

    Other_____

Students would get in trouble less if:

    They had more friends at school   _____

    They followed the rules   _____

    They were stronger academically _____

    They had more support at home   _____

    None of these   _____

    Other_____

What are your thoughts and suggestion(s)? How can the school help these students?

_____

_____

_____

_____

How can the administration or the school community help you work with these students?

_____

_____

_____

_____

KEEPITUP MIDDLE SCHOOL BULLYING SURVEY

Student Survey

Please circle your response to each question. Thank you for your help in understanding bullying and harassment at Keepitup Middle School.

Grade: 7th or 8th
Gender: Female or Male

1. I have been bullied.	Never	Sometimes	Always
2. I have observed others being bullied.	Never	Sometimes	Always
3. I don't have strategies to use if I'm bullied.	Disagree	Sometimes	Agree
4. I would not tell an adult if I were being bullied.	Disagree	Sometimes	Agree
5. I bully other students.	Never	Sometimes	Always
6. I have bullied others by text, IM or e-mail.	Never	Sometimes	Always
7. I have been bullied by text, IM or e-mail.	Never	Sometimes	Always

Share a specific incident of bullying you have observed:

_____

_____

_____

_____

_____

_____

_____

_____

Based on a survey created by Valerie Hardy and Kristen Biernesser

KEEPITUP MIDDLE SCHOOL BULLYING SURVEY

Faculty Survey

Dear Teachers,

Please complete the following questionnaire to help us understand the impact of bullying and harassment at our school and to help us determine the effectiveness of current practices.

1. Do you think bullying is a problem at Keepitup Middle School (KMS)?

    1-No   2-Unsure   3-Yes

2. Have you observed bullying at KMS?

    1-No   2-Unsure   3-Yes

3. Do you know how to report bullying?

    1-No   2-Unsure   3-Yes

4. Are students willing to report incidents of bullying?

    1-No   2-Unsure   3-Yes

5. Do you think that cyber-bullying is a problem at KMS?

    1-No   2-Unsure   3-Yes

6. Do you think parents are aware of cyber-bullying?

    1-No   2-Unsure   3-Yes

Additional comments, concerns and/or suggestions:

_____

_____

_____

_____

_____

_____

_____

_____

Based on a survey created by Valerie Hardy and Kristen Biernesser

MIDDLE SCHOOL NEEDS ASSESSMENT

School Counseling Program Needs Assessment

Name & Team: _____ Date: _____

The school counseling department would like your help in planning the classroom lessons and small-group counseling focus for the coming year. Please read the following directions and provide your feedback.

The following list names various topics that might be addressed in a school counseling program. Rank the 10 topics you feel would be most valuable in terms of your needs, students' needs or the school's needs. Place the number 1 next to the topic you feel is most important; 2 by the next most important and so on to number 10. If you have some suggestions that are not a part of the list, place them in the spaces that have been provided, and include your suggestions in your top-10 rankings.

Please place completed needs assessments in the school counseling department mail box.

_____ Helping students with educational planning, curriculum and choosing courses

_____ Self-awareness and self-concept

_____ Life planning (balancing school, family, friends, leisure, etc.)

_____ Help for special learning needs

_____ Communication skills

_____ Conflict resolution

_____ Peer mediation

_____ Peer pressure

_____ Substance abuse

_____ Anger management

_____ Racism/discrimination

_____ Sexism

_____ Diversity – learning about own and others' cultures

_____ Acculturation and assimilation

_____ Divorce/blended families

_____ Grief

_____ School adjustment

_____ Peer relationships

_____ Assertiveness training

_____ Study skills

_____ Test-taking skills

_____ Organization skills

_____ Time management/ procrastination

_____ Personal safety

_____ Stress management for students

_____ Stress management for teachers

_____ Special enrichment programs (e.g., AVID, CPP, EIP, mentor program)

_____ Excessive absences/tardies

_____ Motivation and goal setting

_____ Bullying

_____ Sexual harassment

_____ Combating negative media messages

_____ Eating disorders/negative body image

_____ Career information

_____ Other _____

Typically, school counseling services are addressed through the direct and indirect service to students and for students. Typical services are listed below. After reading this list, circle the appropriate number to rate the service areas according to the emphasis you feel they should receive in the total school counseling program.

4=Top priority
3=Moderate priority
2=Fairly low priority
1=Very low priority

1. Direct Services to Students:

    4 3 2 1   Classroom lessons

    4 3 2 1   Group counseling

    4 3 2 1   Individual counseling

    4 3 2 1   Individual student planning

    4 3 2 1   Crisis counseling

2. Indirect Services for Students:

    4 3 2 1   Referrals: attendance referrals, referral to community resources, tutoring referrals

    4 3 2 1   Consulting with families with school social worker and school psychologist

    4 3 2 1   Local screening and child study

    4 3 2 1   Conferences with parents/guardians, teachers

    4 3 2 1   Consulting with parents, administrators, school and community specialists

Based on a survey created by Amelia Risner-Butera

EXAMPLE OF A MIDDLE SCHOOL GROUP COUNSELING PRE-/POST-TEST

Resiliency Group: Pre- and Post-Assessment

Directions: Circle the number that best describes how you feel.

1=Strongly Disagree 2=Disagree 3=Undecided 4=Agree 5=Strongly Agree

1. I can manage challenges and/or difficult people or situations.

   1   2   3   4   5

2. I feel I possess strengths that help me to cope with my challenges and/or situations.

   1   2   3   4   5

3. I feel I have people in my life who support me.

   1   2   3   4   5

4. I am able to talk about my feelings with others.

   1   2   3   4   5

5. I am able to ask for help when I need it.

   1   2   3   4   5

Created by Andrea Farrow

EXAMPLE OF A MIDDLE SCHOOL STUDY SKILLS SELF-ASSESSMENT

Check My Skills

	Always 3	Sometimes 2	Never 1
I bring all necessary materials to every class.			
I complete all of my assignments on time.			
I turn in all of my assignments on time.			
I write down all of my assignments in my agenda.			
I ask questions in class when I don't understand something.			
I check Blackboard for clarification when I am unsure of an assignment.			
I use Lion Time to complete work or to get help from teachers.			
I stay after school when I need additional academic support.			
I study for tests ahead of time.			
I plan ahead and complete long-term assignments in steps.			
My materials are well-organized in binders or folders.			
I have a place, time and materials to study at home.			

Add It Up = _____

STATUS
31-36: OMG (On My Game)
24-30: TMI (Try Minor Improvements)
23 or less: #GTG (Got To Grow)

Created by Shirley Alvarez, Paula Cotman, Rachel Haney and Debbie McDonald, 2012

EXAMPLE OF A SCHOOL COUNSELING PRESENTATION EVALUATION

Freshmen PSAT Interpretation

Please complete this evaluation of the PSAT Interpretation presentation.

1. Before the presentation, did you know how to read your PSAT score report?

   1-no   2- somewhat   3-yes

2. Now that the presentation is complete, do you have a better understanding of your PSAT score report?

   1-no   2- no change in my understanding   3-yes

3. Was the presentation clear and easy to follow?

   1- no   2- somewhat   3-yes

4. Do you plan to go back and review the questions in the test booklet, now that you have your answers?

   1- no   2- unsure   3-yes

5. Do you have any additional comments?

   _____

   _____

   _____

   _____

   _____

   _____

   _____

   _____

Based on survey created by Renee Service, Tiffany Haddock and Jill Wilson

JUNIOR CAREER UNIT SURVEY

Students, please complete the following survey about your recent visit to the Career Center.

1. Have you visited the Career Center before today?
   a. No
   b. Once or twice
   c. I've been to the Career Center a few times but not regularly
   d. I visit the Career Center regularly

2. Do you feel you have a better understanding of what is available to you through the Career Center after today's lesson?
   a. No
   b. Unsure
   c. There is no change in my understanding of what's available in the Career Center
   d. Yes

3. Will you visit the Career Center more after today's lesson?
   a. No
   b. Unsure
   c. Probably
   d. Yes

4. Do you have a better understanding of how to use the career Web-based program that was administered today?
   a. No
   b. Unsure
   c. There is no change in my understanding
   d. Yes

5. Will you use the Web-based career program more after today's lesson?
   a. Yes
   b. No
   c. Not sure/maybe

6. Did you find the results of the Web-based interest inventory to be accurate?
   a. No
   b. Unsure
   c. Somewhat
   d. Yes

7. Will you use the results of the Web-based interest inventory to help you with your career and college planning?
   a. No
   b. I did not finish the inventory
   c. Somewhat
   d. Yes

Based on a survey created by Renee Service

HIGH SCHOOL SURVEY PRE-/POST-TEST

Senior Survey Pre-Test

Name _____ English Period/Teacher _____

How prepared do you feel to apply to complete:

	Poor	Fair	Satisfactory	Good	Excellent
School searches	☐	☐	☐	☐	☐
College application process	☐	☐	☐	☐	☐
Scholarships/ financial aid forms	☐	☐	☐	☐	☐
College essays	☐	☐	☐	☐	☐
Career/major choices	☐	☐	☐	☐	☐

What other concerns about college and career readiness do you have?

_____

_____

_____

_____

_____

_____

Check box if you are interested in participating in a college preparation group ☐

Senior Survey Post-Test

Name _____ English Period/Teacher _____

**How prepared do you now feel having participated
in a college preparation group?:**

	Poor	Fair	Satisfactory	Good	Excellent
School searches	☐	☐	☐	☐	☐
College application process	☐	☐	☐	☐	☐
Scholarships/ financial aid forms	☐	☐	☐	☐	☐
College essays	☐	☐	☐	☐	☐
Career/major choices	☐	☐	☐	☐	☐

How could the groups be improved?

_____

_____

_____

_____

_____

_____

Created by Julie Chen, 2012

DATA Report Examples

D ESIGN

Approximately 40 percent of the 160 disciplinary referrals at Somewhere Elementary School are for sixth-grader misbehavior.

The purpose: The school counselor has collected perception data about the issue. Based on that data the school counselor uses group counseling with the sixth-grade students who have received more than three disciplinary referrals. The purpose of the groups will be to increase sense of support, coping and friendship skills.

The goal: To decrease discipline incidents for identified sixth-graders (having three or more discipline incidents) by 50 percent and increase academic achievement average by 50 percent.

A SK

■ **Record review:** Ten students were identified for the group based on having three or more discipline referrals (for a total of 54 for the group of 10 students) and one or more D or F grade.

■ **Outcome data:** Students' January and June report card grades and behavioral marks will be compared, and student discipline referrals before and after the group will be compared. (Academic grades in four subjects and behavior grades U, S, O will be converted to numerical grades 1, 2, 3).

■ **Perception data:** Students will complete a pre-post survey before and after the group. Survey questions on a four-point Likert scale (strongly disagree to strongly agree): Teachers help me; I like to come to school; I have friends at school; I believe doing well in school is important.

TRACK

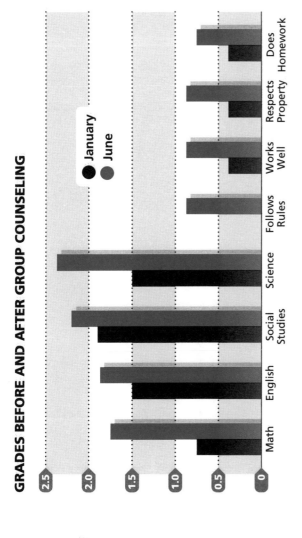

GRADES BEFORE AND AFTER GROUP COUNSELING

● January
● June

Math English Social Studies Science Follows Rules Works Well Respects Property Does Homework

2.5 2.0 1.5 1.0 0.5 0

- Average GPA went from 1.38 to 2.06 comparing January to June grades for a 56 percent change.

- Number of referrals for group dropped from 56 to 25 for an 80 percent change.

- Behavioral grades increased from .30 to .80 for a 60 percent change.

- Perception data indicated an average increase of 50 percent improvement on all four survey items. Students comments: "I liked being in the group." "School is more fun." "My teachers are helping me more."

ANNOUNCE

- Small group counseling was successful. Discipline referrals for this group are down, grades and behavioral marks have improved.

- Share results with administrators and teachers.

- Consider what other factors are interfering with student achievement such as teacher beliefs.

- Compare the data from group members to students not participating in the group; consider increasing the number of groups.

Welcome Elementary School DATA Report

D ESIGN

Peer mediation is an alternative problem-solving strategy used at Welcome Elementary School. Training for new peer mediators is held every spring with selected fifth-graders.

Question: Does participating in peer mediation training improve a student's communication and problem-solving skills?

A SK

- Twenty fifth-grade students were selected for peer mediation training (eight sessions) and were given a pre- and post-test to measure the benefits of training including: their sense of self, communication skills with friends, their ability to help solve their own conflicts and the conflicts of others. This assessment was used to compare the students' self-perception before and after training.

- A five-point scale was used to answer the seven questions:

- Strongly disagree (1) Disagree (2) Not sure (3) Agree (4) Strongly agree (5)

- Total scores for each question were averaged for both pre- and post-test scores.

IMPACT OF PEER MEDIATION TRAINING

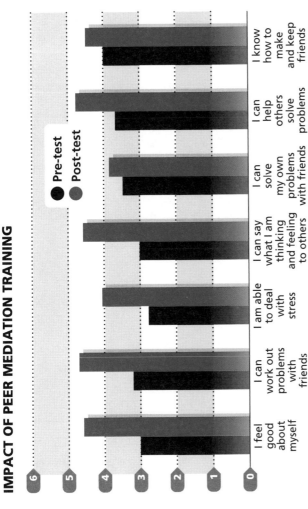

- Pre-test
- Post-test

As a result of peer mediation training sense of self improved by 53 percent; ability to work out problems with friends increased by 47 percent; ability to deal with stress increased by 48 percent; ability to express self increased by 53 percent; ability to solve problems increased by 29 percent; ability to solve problems of others increased by 30 percent; ability to make and keep friends increased by 25 percent.

Implications/Recommendations:

- Continue peer mediation training.
- Share results with administration, teachers and parents.
- Examine achievement data to determine whether peer mediation training has an impact.
- Survey others concerning the impact of mediation such as teachers and disputants.
- Consider providing peer mediation training to other student groups such as the safety patrol or student leaders.

Summary: Peer mediation training helped students in a variety of ways including increased sense of self, ability to solve problems for self and others, ability to deal with stress and make and keep friends.

Mistry Middle School DATA Report • November 2012

D ESIGN

Purpose: The purpose of this investigation was to find out how the school counseling program could support academically unsuccessful middle school students.

Burning question: What are the perceptions of academically unsuccessful middle school students concerning the supportive climate at Mistry Middle School?

A SK

Surveys were given to 50 seventh- and eighth-grade students, all who had two or more D/F's on their interim report. Students were asked to respond on a five-point Likert scale about their perception of the academic support they receive at school and at home, as well as one open-ended question.

MISTRY MIDDLE SCHOOL STUDENT SUCCESS DATA

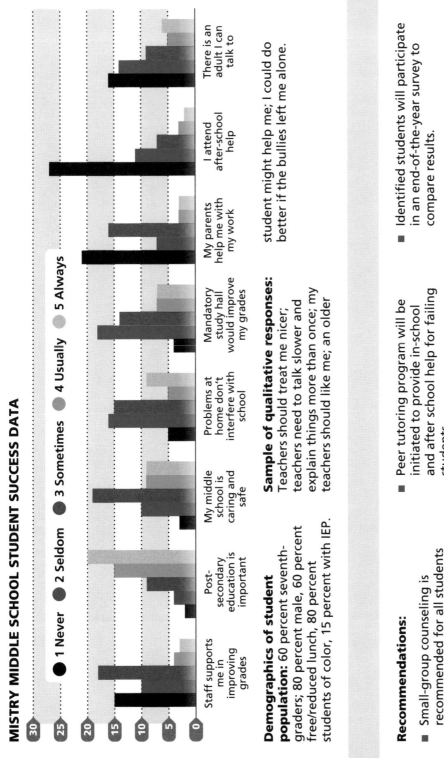

● 1 Never ● 2 Seldom ● 3 Sometimes ● 4 Usually ● 5 Always

Categories: Staff supports me in improving grades; Post-secondary education is important; My middle school is caring and safe; Problems at home don't interfere with school; Mandatory study hall would improve my grades; My parents help me with my work; I attend after-school help; There is an adult I can talk to

Demographics of student population: 60 percent seventh-graders; 80 percent male, 60 percent free/reduced lunch, 80 percent students of color, 15 percent with IEP.

Sample of qualitative responses: Teachers should treat me nicer; teachers need to talk slower and explain things more than once; my teachers should like me; an older student might help me; I could do better if the bullies left me alone.

TRACK

ANNOUNCE

Recommendations:

- Small-group counseling is recommended for all students receiving more than one D/F grade.
- Faculty workshops should be held to examine the findings to examine school climate.

- Peer tutoring program will be initiated to provide in-school and after school help for failing students.
- Student grades will be monitored at the end of the second marking period and compared with first marking-period grades.
- Identified students will participate in an end-of-the-year survey to compare results.

Mistry Middle School DATA Report • June 2013

D ESIGN

Purpose: The purpose of this investigation was to find out how the school counseling program could support academically unsuccessful middle school students.

Burning question: What are the perceptions of academically unsuccessful middle school students concerning the supportive climate at Mistry Middle School?

Goal: Identified students with one or more failing grade for the first interim will decrease failing grades by 50 percent by June 2013.

A SK

- Fifty students with one or more D/F grade were identified. The total number of D/F grades: 78.

- Surveys were given to 50 seventh- and eighth-grade students, all who had two or more D/F's on their interim report. Students were asked to respond on a five-point Likert scale concerning their perception of the academic support they receive at school and at home, as well as one open-ended question.

- Interventions included small-group counseling, parent meeting, peer tutoring and bullying initiative.

MISTRY MIDDLE SCHOOL OUTCOME DATA

● D Grade
● F Grade

Outcome data: In November 2012, 50 students earned 78 D/F grades. By June 2013 total number of D/F grades was 46, for a decrease of 30 percent of failing grades.

Perception data: 50 percent of students do not feel staff supports them; 70 percent think post-secondary plans are important; 60 percent say they don't have an adult to help them.

Sample of qualitative responses: Teachers should treat me nicer; teachers need to talk slower and explain things more than once; my teachers should like me; an older student might help me; I could do better if the bullies left me alone.

Recommendations:

■ Small-group counseling should be implemented for all students receiving more than one D/F grade.

■ Faculty workshops should be held to examine the findings about school climate.

■ Questionnaires will be given to students on the A/B honor roll to compare results.

■ Student grades will be monitored at the end of the second marking period and compared with first marking-period grades.

■ Identified students will participate in an end-of-the-year survey to compare perception data results.

Manager Middle School DATA Report • Spring 2013

DESIGN

Review of school data indicates a group of 20 students have one or more D/Fs after the first quarter. This pattern has been repeated for the last two years. Individual conferences with students and parents have been tried but with minimal effect.

SMART Goal: Identified seventh-grade students with one or more D/F in a core class at the end of first quarter will improve their average GPA by 50 percent by the end of second quarter.

ASK

- Twenty students were identified for the small-group counseling sessions. Ten students participated during the second semester (10 parents gave permission).

- Students took part in six small-group counseling sessions during Cougar Paws class (15-30 minutes).

- The group sessions covered topics including locker, book bag and home organization; keeping track of assignments; managing time; creating a productive home and school environment; attitude toward school; and personal goal setting.

- Data collected compare pre- and post-GPAs and the number of D/F's earned.

- GPAs and number of D/F's were compared between 10 students who participated in group counseling and 10 students who did not.

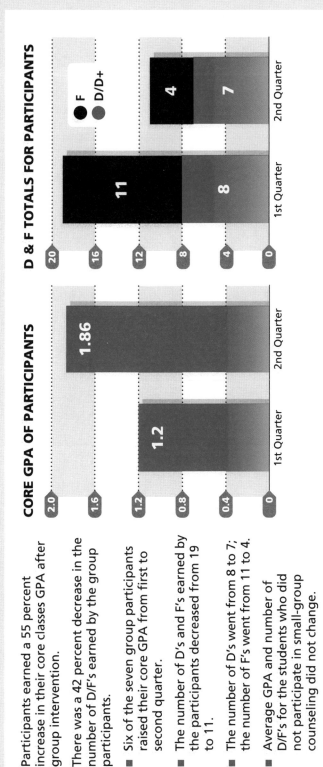

CORE GPA OF PARTICIPANTS

- 2.0
- 1.6
- 1.2
- 0.8
- 0.4
- 0

1.2 — 1st Quarter
1.86 — 2nd Quarter

D & F TOTALS FOR PARTICIPANTS

● F
● D/D+

- 20
- 16
- 12
- 8
- 4
- 0

1st Quarter: **11**, **8**
2nd Quarter: **4**, **7**

T RACK

Participants earned a 55 percent increase in their core classes GPA after group intervention.

There was a 42 percent decrease in the number of D/F's earned by the group participants.

- Six of the seven group participants raised their core GPA from first to second quarter.

- The number of D's and F's earned by the participants decreased from 19 to 11.

- The number of D's went from 8 to 7; the number of F's went from 11 to 4.

- Average GPA and number of D/F's for the students who did not participate in small-group counseling did not change.

A NNOUNCE

As a result of the group counseling the following implications and recommendations can be made:

- Group participants self-reported they better understood how to use the organizational tools available to them at school.

- Participants should continue to take part in the study-skills group if needed, and new participants should be identified from the following quarter interims.

- Findings should be shared with administrators, teachers and parents.

- Due to success of this intervention, increasing the time and total number of groups to accommodate more academically struggling students should be considered.

D ESIGN

Purpose: Anywhere High School is located in an urban setting with less than 30 percent of the student population enrolled in an honors, AP/IB or dual enrollment course. The school counselors are working collaboratively with the principal and teachers to eliminate barriers that contribute to declining or sustained enrollment in honors, AP/IB and dual enrollment.

Goal: To increase student enrollment in honors, AP/IB or dual enrollment by 10 percent for the current school year.

A SK

The following procedures will be used to increase enrollment.

■ Conduct records review of a random sample of ninth- to 11th-grade students to determine the demographic profile of students currently enrolled.

■ Develop and administer survey to random sample ninth- to 11th-grade students prior to academic advisement/registration orientations for the upcoming school year. The survey will consist of Likert-scale statements. Results will be disaggregated and shared.

T RACK

10TH GRADE FINDINGS

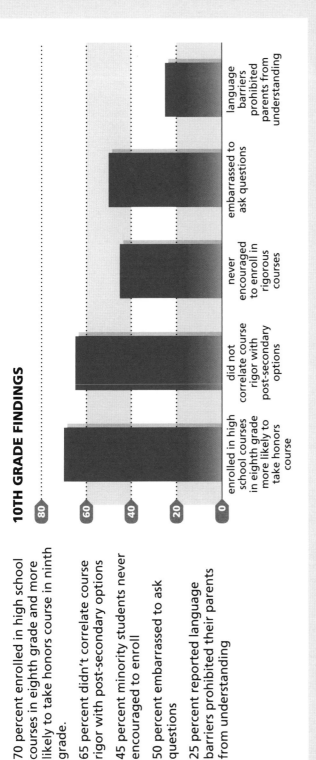

- 70 percent enrolled in high school courses in eighth grade and more likely to take honors course in ninth grade.
- 65 percent didn't correlate course rigor with post-secondary options
- 45 percent minority students never encouraged to enroll
- 50 percent embarrassed to ask questions
- 25 percent reported language barriers prohibited their parents from understanding

A NNOUNCE

- Create schoolwide mentoring culture promoting college readiness.
- Share results of survey with staff; explore strategies to increase student enrollment.
- Translate all materials intended for parental action into multiple languages, and distribute multiple ways.

Recommendations:

- Schedule middle and high school counselor/administrator collaboration meetings to discuss vertical academic/career articulation strategies.

DATA Report created by Maria Rosario

Fasttrack High School DATA Report • Fall 2013
Gaining Early Access and Readiness for Undergraduate Program (GEAR UP) After-School Tutoring Intervention

D ESIGN

Goal:
GEAR UP program students receiving any D/F grades at first interim will increase GPA by .5 by the end of the first quarter.

A SK

Data Collection:

- Nine students' GPAs were monitored based on the first six sessions of tutorial program.

- Data report compares progress based on GPA on first interim grades (pre-test) and first-quarter grades (post-test).

- Total D's and F's were also monitored.

- A survey was administrated to identified students to collect perceptions of the impact of the GEAR UP program.

GEAR UP STUDENTS' GPA

● 1st Qtr. Interim GPA
● 1st Qtr. GPA

Student: A B C D E F G H I

(y-axis: 3.0, 2.5, 2.0, 1.5, 1.0, 0.5, 0)

The following data were obtained based on six tutorial intervention sessions and the students' responses from a questionnaire:

D & F TOTALS

● F's
● D's

1st Interim: 18, 7
1st Grading: 11, 13

(y-axis: 30, 25, 20, 15, 10, 5, 0)

- 33 percent of students increased their GPA.

- The amount of F's earned by students decreased from 18 to 11.

- 88 percent of students agreed the GEAR UP program motivated them to do better at school.

- 100 percent of students recognized the importance of pursuing higher education after high school.

- 55 percent of students felt indifferent about their ability to concentrate in school work due to problems at home and/or in the community.

- 88 percent of students agreed the tutorial program helped them improve their grades.

- 100 percent felt fortunate to be part of the GEAR UP program.

- 100 percent of students believe the GEAR UP program will help them find colleges after they graduate.

As a result of the data, the following implications and recommendations are addressed:

- The tutoring intervention program has shown improvement on students' GPAs and should continue for greater results.

- Strongly recommend at-risk students participate regularly in the tutorial program.

- Encourage high-achiever students to participate in the tutorial program for enrichment.

- Follow up on students' attendance, and reward students who participate regularly.

- Maintain a close relationship and open communication with students, parents and teachers.

- Share data with administrators, school counselors, teachers, tutors, GEAR UP career coach and coordinator.

DESIGN

Purpose:
Showmehow Secondary School is known for its academic reputation; however, there is concern for the group of students who do not have a clear post-graduation plan and continue to move through high school with only average or below-average grades. Through a small-group intervention, we hope to connect students with a career goal and increase GPAs and likelihood of high school graduation.

Goal:
Identified students will identify career interests and post-high-school plans and increase GPA by 1.0 by the end of the school year.

ASK

Process data: After a records review, six ninth- and 10th-grade students with a 2.4 GPA or lower who had not identified a career goal or a post-secondary plan were invited to participate in the group.

Perception data: Students completed a pre-test asking about the various segments of high school life at their school (academics, activities, sports, social, school involvement, plans and goals, etc.) to determine group topics. A post-test evaluation was used to assess group benefits.

Outcome data: January GPA was compared with June GPA. The group met for six sessions over three months. The meetings were: introduction and purpose, career assessment and trip preparation, academy visit, academy wrap-up, career center visit and closing.

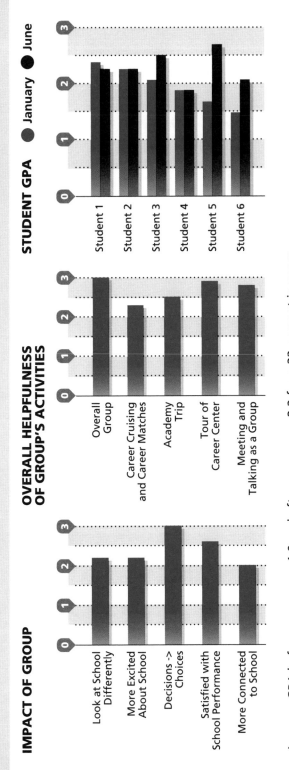

IMPACT OF GROUP

- Look at School Differently
- More Excited About School
- Decisions -> Choices
- Satisfied with School Performance
- More Connected to School

OVERALL HELPFULNESS OF GROUP'S ACTIVITIES

- Overall Group
- Career Cruising and Career Matches
- Academy Trip
- Tour of Career Center
- Meeting and Talking as a Group

STUDENT GPA ● January ● June

- Student 1
- Student 2
- Student 3
- Student 4
- Student 5
- Student 6

Average GPA before group was 1.9 and after group was 2.3 for a 22 percent increase.

Implications:
Group counseling had an impact on academic achievement, student engagement and career planning.

Recommendations: Share findings with the school counselors, career specialist and the student services director.
Increase small group counseling opportunities for at-risk students.

Based on a DATA Report by Robin Huppeth

D ESIGN

The research question:
What are the factors contributing to the number of students receiving D's and F's at Fortune High School?

A SK

Data-collection strategies:

- All 488 students on the D/F list attended a seminar and were surveyed about their perceptions of what contributed to their poor grades.

- The faculty and staff were also surveyed concerning their perceptions of student failure.

- The surveys was administered to A/B honor roll students to compare the results of the two student surveys.

Outcome data:

- The number of students on the D/F list was reduced by 2 percent each of four consecutive marking periods.
- There was a 9 percent increase in application to post-secondary programs.

Perception data: Students say that they wish teachers...

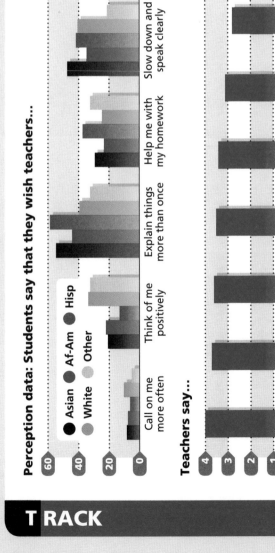

Legend: ● Asian ● Af-Am ● Hisp ● White ● Other

Categories (with scale 0, 20, 40, 60): Call on me more often · Think of me positively · Explain things more than once · Help me with my homework · Slow down and speak clearly

Teachers say...

Categories (with scale 0, 1, 2, 3, 4): Lack of motivation · No homework · Attendance · Parental support · Lack of basic skills · Language proficiency · Class size

Initial findings from the D/F student surveys were shared with administrators and teachers.

Implications and recommendations:

- School counselors can be catalysts for change, can take action and can influence stakeholders.
- All of this has led to discussions about how belief systems affect student success.
- Diversity training will benefit faculty and staff.
- This is a process, and only the first steps have been taken to understand and address the core issues.

D ESIGN

Purpose: Bowman High School counselors have implemented college preparation lessons and activities to students leading up to their senior year. Interest and participation in such programs have been minimal. Bowman High School does not have a career/ college counselor to help students through the process.

Question: How prepared do seniors feel to complete college search/ application, college essay, financial aid/ scholarships and career/major choices?

A SK

The following procedures will be used to investigate this issue:

■ 623 seniors were given a needs assessment in their English classrooms in September following a school counseling curriculum lesson.

■ The needs assessment consisted of five questions (How prepared do you feel to complete college searches/application, essays, financial aid/scholarships and career/ major choices?) using a Likert scale (poor-fair-satisfactory-good-excellent). The needs assessment also asked students if they would like to participate in a small group with the school counselor in their area of concern.

■ An open-ended question was included in the survey.

HOW PREPARED DO YOU FEEL TO COMPLETE PARTS OF THE COLLEGE PROCESS?

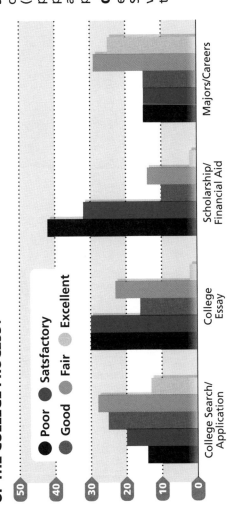

● Poor ● Satsfactory
● Good ● Fair ● Excellent

College Search/Application • College Essay • Scholarship/Financial Aid • Majors/Careers

0 · 10 · 20 · 30 · 40 · 50

Student Summary Findings:
Students felt the least prepared to complete scholarship/financial aid (42 percent of students felt poorly prepared), college essays (30 percent poor), majors/careers (15 percent poor) and college search/applications (14 percent poor).

Open-ended Responses: Students expressed a lot of support was needed. Some students were concerned about whether college was a good fit for them.

Share findings and results with administration and faculty for input and to emphasize the educational impact:

■ Consider the demographic data (ethnicity, gender, FARMS, SES).

■ What would the impact of a college/career counselor be at the school?

■ Consider how offering parent workshops, group counseling and classroom lessons might address the need for additional support to students on the college process.

■ What lessons and information need to be given to students prior to senior year to help them feel more comfortable with the process? Examine current practices and school counseling curriculum lessons used for freshman, sophomores and juniors on college/career preparedness.

■ How can teachers assist students with areas of the process such as essays?

■ Can additional parent workshops/seminars help parents assist their children?

■ Student needs assesment at the start of the school year should determine the groups or resources.

DATA Report by Julie Chen

D ESIGN

Purpose: Seniors at Bowman High School indicated on a needs assessment at the start of the year they needed more assistance in the scholarship/financial aid process when preparing for the college-going process. Small-group sessions were created to address students' needs.

Question: Do Bowman High School seniors feel better prepared for the college process after participating in the scholarship/financial aid group?

A SK

- 623 seniors were given a five-question needs assessment in September on preparedness for college search/application, essays, financial aid/scholarships and career/major choices.

- Students who marked "Poor" in preparation were invited to attend one of 12 interactive sessions to assist them with the financial aid process and scholarship search in the computer lab.

- Students attended a 30-minute session during a time period that did not interfere with academic instruction.

- Exit questionnaires were given to all group participants to assess if they felt more prepared to complete scholarships and financial aid after participating in the group session.

- Students were also able to mark on the exit questionnaire if they needed additional assistance and had other questions or comments regarding scholarships/financial aid.

T RACK

HOW PREPARED DO YOU FEEL TO APPLY FOR SCHOLARSHIPS OR FINANCIAL AID?

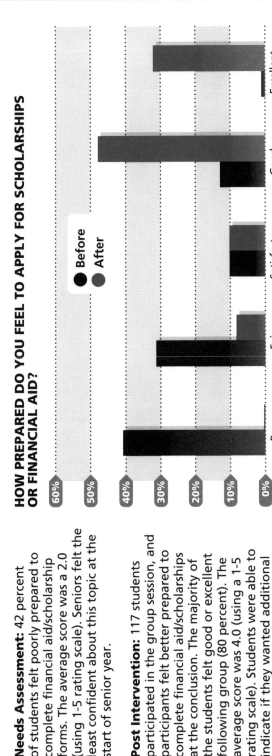

- Before
- After

(y-axis: 60%, 50%, 40%, 30%, 20%, 10%, 0%)

(x-axis categories: Poor, Fair, Satisfactory, Good, Excellent)

Needs Assessment: 42 percent of students felt poorly prepared to complete financial aid/scholarship forms. The average score was a 2.0 (using 1-5 rating scale). Seniors felt the least confident about this topic at the start of senior year.

Post Intervention: 117 students participated in the group session, and participants felt better prepared to complete financial aid/scholarships at the conclusion. The majority of the students felt good or excellent following group (80 percent). The average score was 4.0 (using a 1-5 rating scale). Students were able to indicate if they wanted additional support or help with the process.

A NNOUNCE

- ■ Track data on students who apply to college and apply for financial aid.
- ■ Consider how offering parent workshops, group counseling and classroom lessons might address the need for additional support to students on the college process.
- ■ What lessons and information need to be given to students prior to senior year to help them feel more comfortable with the process?
- ■ Examine current practices for freshman, sophomores and juniors or college and career preparedness.
- ■ Student needs assessment at the start of the school year should determine student needs.

Share findings and results with administration and faculty for input and to emphasize the educational impact:

- ■ Consider demographic data (ethnicity, gender, FARMS, SES, first family member to attend college).
- ■ What would the impact of a college/ career counselor be at BHS?

DATA report created by Julie Chen

PART VI

References, Recommended Reading and Websites

References

American School Counselor Association [ASCA] (2005). *The ASCA National Model: A framework for school counseling programs* (2nd ed.). Alexandria, VA: Author.

American School Counselor Association [ASCA] (2012). *The ASCA National Model: A framework for school counseling programs* (3rd. ed.). Alexandria, VA: Author.

Bailey, D. F., Getch, Y. Q., & Chen-Hayes, S. (2007). Achievement advocacy for all students through transformative school counseling programs. In B.T. Erford (Ed.), *Transforming the school counseling profession* (2nd ed., pp. 98-120). Upper Saddle River, NJ: Pearson Education.

Bauman, S. (2004) School counselors and research revisited. *Professional School Counseling, 7,* 141-151.

Brigman, G. A, Webb, L. D, & Campbell, C. (2007). Building skills for school success: Improving the academic and social competence of students. *Professional School Counseling, 10,* 279-288.

Brooks-McNamara, V., & Pederson, L. (2006). Practitioner inquiry: A method to advocate for systemic change. *Professional School Counseling, 9,* 257-261.

Carey J., Harrity J., & Dimmit C. (2005). The development of a self-assessment instrument to measure a school district's readiness to implement the ASCA National Model. *Professional School Counseling, 8,* 305-312.

Denzin, N. & Lincoln, Y. (2011). *Handbook of Qualitative Research* (3rd ed.). Thousand Oaks, CA: Corwin Press.

Dillman, D. A. (2007). *Mail and internet surveys. The tailored design* (2nd ed., 2007 Update). Hoboken, NJ: Wiley.

Dimmitt, C. (2009). Why evaluation matters: Determining effective school counseling practices. *Professional School Counseling, 12,* 395-399.

Dimmitt, C., Carey, J., & Hatch, T. (2007). *Evidence-based school counseling: Making a difference with data-driven practices.* Thousand Oaks, CA: Corwin Press.

Dollarhide, C., & Lemberger, M. E. (2006). "No Child Left Behind:" Implications for school counselors. *Professional School Counseling, 9,* 295-304.

Fraenkel, J. R., & Walle, N. E. (2000). *How to design & evaluate research in education.* Boston, MA: McGraw Hill.

Fraenkel, J. R., & Wallen, N. E. (2009). *How to design and evaluate research in education* (4th ed). New York, NY: McGraw-Hill.

Gilchrist, S. (2007). S.O.A.R.I.N.G. In C. Holcomb-McCoy, *School counseling to close the achievement gap: A social justice framework for success* (pp. 89-91). Thousand Oaks, CA: Corwin Press.

Gillies, R. M. (1993). Action research for school counselors. *School Counselor, 41,* 69-72.

Guiffrida, D. A., Douthit, K. Z., Lynch, M. F., & Mackie, K. L. (2011). Publishing action research in counseling journals. *Journal of Counseling & Development, 89,* 282-295.

Haycock, K. (2001). Closing the achievement gap. *Educational Leadership, 58,* 6-11.

Holcomb-McCoy, C. (2007). *School counseling to close the achievement gap: A social justice framework for success.* Thousand Oaks, CA: Corwin Press.

Isaacs, M. L. (2003). Data-driven decision making: The engine of accountability. *Professional School Counseling, 6,* 288-295.

McDonough, P.M. (2004). Choosing colleges: How social class and school structure opportunity. Albany, NY: State University of New York Press.

No Child Left Behind Act of 2001. Retrieved March 20, 2013 from http://www2.ed.gov/policy/elsec/leg/esea02/beginning.html#sec1.

Patton, M. Q. (2002). *Qualitative research & evaluation methods* (3rd ed.). Thousand Oaks, CA: Sage.

Poynton, T. A., & Baker, T. D. (2007). Free tech tools. *ASCA School Counselor, 44*, 22-29.

Rowell, L. L. (2005). Collaborative action research and school counselors. *Professional School Counseling, 9*, 28-36.

Rowell, L. L. (2006). Action research and school counseling: Closing the gap between research and practice. *Professional School Counseling, 9*, 376-384.

Rubin, A. (2008). *Practitioner's guide to using research for evidence-based practice.* John Wiley & Sons, Inc: New Jersey.

S. 844--112th Congress: Race to the Top Act of 2011. (2011). In www.GovTrack.us. Retrieved March 4, 2013, from http://www.govtrack.us/congress/bills/112/s844

Schwandt, T. (2007). *The sage dictionary of qualitative inquiry* (3rd ed.). Thousand Oaks, CA: Sage.

Singleton, G. E., & Linton, C. (2006). *Courageous conversations about race.* Thousand Oaks, CA: Corwin Press.

Stone, C. B., & Dahir, C. A. (2013). *School counselor accountability: A MEASURE of student success* (3rd ed.). Upper Saddle River, NJ: Pearson.

Young, A., & Kaffenberger, C. (2009). *Making DATA work* (2nd ed.). Alexandria, VA: American School Counselor Association.

Young, A., & Kaffenberger, C. (2011). The beliefs and practices of school counselors who use data to implement comprehensive school counseling programs. *Professional School Counseling, 15*, 67-76.

Readings and Resources

American School Counselor Association (2007). *ASCA School Counselor, 44*(3). Practitioner Research: The fabric of a sound program.

DeVellis, R. F. (2012). *Scale development: Theory and applications.* Thousand Oaks, CA: Sage Publications.

Fowler, F. J. (1995). *Improving survey questions.* Thousand Oaks, CA: Sage Publications.

Fraenkel, J. R., & Wallen, N. E. (2009). *How to design and evaluate research in education* (4th ed). New York, NY: McGraw-Hill.

House, R. M., & Martin, P. J. (1998). Advocating for better futures for all students: A new vision for school counselors. *Education, 119,* 284-291.

Kaffenberger, C. (2012). What does it mean to have a data-driven school counseling program? In *ASCA National Model: A framework for school counseling programs* (3rd ed.; pp.117-119). Alexandria, VA: American School Counselor Association.

Kaffenberger, C., & Young, A. (2007). Data is not a four-letter word. *ASCA School Counselor, 44,* 16-21.

Marzano (2006). *What works in schools: Translating research in action.* Alexandria, VA: Author.

Poynton, T. A., & Carey, J. C. (2006). An integrated model of data-based decision making for schools counseling. *Professional School Counseling, 10,* 121-130.

Sagor, R. (2011). *The action research guidebook* (2nd ed.). Thousand Oaks, CA: Corwin Press.

Singleton, G. E., & Linton, C. (2006). *Courageous conversations about race.* Thousand Oaks, CA: Corwin Press.

Strauss, A. L., & Corbin, J. (1994). Grounded theory methodology: An interview. In N. K. Denzin & Y. S. Lincoln (Eds.), *Handbook of qualitative research* (2nd ed.). Thousand Oaks: Sage Publications.

Willis, G. B. (2005). *Cognitive interviewing: A tool for improving questionnaire design.* Thousand Oak, CA: Sage Publications.

Websites

American School Counselor Association
www.schoolcounselor.org

The Center for School Counseling Outcome Research
www.umass.edu/schoolcounseling

The Education Trust
www.edtrust.org
(Go to Data Tools and Presentations, and select data presentations)

EZAnalyze
www.ezanalyze.com

National Center for Educational Statistics
http://nces.ed.gov
(Search: students' classroom)

Naviance
www.naviance.com

National Office of School Counselor Advocacy (NOSCA), The College Board
www.collegeboard.org

Survey Monkey
www.surveymonkey.com

Tools for School Improvement Planning
www.annenberginstitute.org/tools/index.php